Mr. Helge B. Olsen
1628 Redwood Ln
Davis, CA 95616

Mr. Helge B. Olsen
1628 Redwood Ln
Davis, CA 95616

VENICE
HIDDEN SPLENDORS

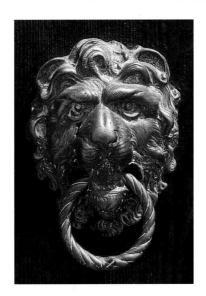

Cesare M. Cunaccia

Photography by
Mark E. Smith

VENICE
HIDDEN SPLENDORS

Introduction by
Roberto De Feo

Flammarion
Paris - New York

Acknowledgements

I would like to express my thanks to both my publishers, who enabled me to embark on this adventure,
and to all those who so kindly allowed photographs to be taken.
Among the many people who made this book possible, giving freely of their time and invaluable suggestions,
I would like to record particular thanks to the Contessa Cecilia Giustiniani Recanati,
the Nobildonna Cecilia Giustiniani Collalto Falck, Barone Ernesto Rubin de Cervin and the
Nobildonna Maria Donà dalle Rose Franchin for their many kindnesses.
Special thanks are also due to my friends Elisabetta Jannello Campbell, Elena Barbalich, Piero Pazzi,
Girolamo Marcello and Cinzia Boscolo for all they have done to make this venture a success.
Last but not least, I would like to make particular mention of Roberto De Feo, both for his inestimable
scientific input and for standing selflessly and critically by as the text was being drafted.

Cesare M. Cunaccia

Page 1: Door knocker in the shape of a lion's head
Frontispiece: Decorated door from the Palazzo Barbarigo (see p. 86)
Page 6: View from the bell tower of the Church of San Giorgio Maggiore

Originally published as *Interni a Venezia*, by Cesare M. Cunaccia,
Photography by Mark E. Smith. Copyright © 1994 Arsenale Editrice, Venice.

Other photographs courtesy of:
Archivio Fotografico Osvaldo Böhm (pp. 20-21, 40-41)
Dida Biggi (pp. 112-113)
Cameraphoto (p. 26)
Studio Fotografico Francesco Turio Böhm (pp. 58-59)

General introduction, chapter introductions, and Visitor's Guide
translated by Bridget Mason, all other texts translated by Bernard Wooding.
Index compiled by Emily Wanger

Typeset by Octavo Editions, Paris
Printed and bound by
EBS Editoriale Botolazzi Stei, Verona

Flammarion
26, Rue Racine
75006 Paris

ISBN: 2-08013-573-2
N° d'édition: 0812
Dépôt légal: September 1994
Printed in Italy

CONTENTS

INTRODUCTION

Venice is the most frequently
"portrayed" city in the world.
Alberto Savinio

I t is almost inevitable that in a city like Venice, where the only means of getting
around is on foot or by the slow motorboats and vaporetti, one's gaze is frequently
captured by the astonishing and harmonious perspectives that succeed each other
without interruption.

The Venetians' whole way of life has been shaped by living in an atmosphere
untainted by fast, irritating traffic, and they have always allowed themselves the luxury
of looking around them: they have so much more time at their disposal and make the
most of it to gaze about them as they move from place to place. There are hardly any
harsh or inappropriate reminders of contemporary civilization—no aseptic architecture, no neon signs, no parked cars blocking the way—which means that they can
feast their eyes without interruption. They are well aware of their good fortune as
regards their environment, which is marred only by the entrances to the station at
Santa Lucia and the ugly Piazzale Roma, and they maintain that they could never live
anywhere else in the whole world. Venetians live in a *hortus conclusus*, made up of
campi, *campielli*, *calli*, houses, palaces and churches which all gradually seem to assume
the same proportions, all part of an exquisite and quite unique microcosm where every
humble brick and precious piece of marble is testament to the incommensurable and
varied past which they have been allowed to colonize and perpetuate. In fact, not
much has changed since Henry James wrote in *The Aspern Papers*, "Without streets and
vehicles, the uproar of wheels, the brutality of horses, and with its little winding ways
where people crowd together, where voices sound as in the corridors of a house, where
human step circulates as if it skirted the angles of furniture and shoes never wear out,
the place has the character of an immense collective apartment, in which Piazza San
Marco is the most ornamented corner, and palaces and churches, for the rest, play the
part of great divans of repose, tables of entertainment, expanses of decoration."

But, for us, as for even the most abstracted visitors arriving in Venice, once we
have gotten over the initial moments of disconcertation and facile enthusiasm, we
begin to submerge ourselves in the city, eager to absorb as much as possible of such a
unique place, both physically and spiritually, anxious to capture the soul of Venice.
Not content with the extraordinary variety of the architecture, the Gothic and Renaissance cornices, the decorated capitals, the gently crumbling plasterwork of the façades
resting on the stone pavings where even one's step seems to glide more softly along the
asphalt, we peer timidly into one of the countless churches that are dotted about the

maze of *calli* which form theatrical backdrops to the *campi* that bear their name. Our initial reaction is muted: the half-darkness musty with the lingering scent of incense and candle wax limits our perceptions of what is to come once our eyes have grown accustomed to the light: the glitter of gold, the geometry of the vaults, the shapes of the tombs and the altars, the crêpey protruding stucco work, the colors of the altar pieces and the magnificence of the frescoed ceilings.

Unfortunately the majority of the itineraries concentrate on the most famous monuments or on those that just happen to find themselves on the more popular Venetian "tourist" routes, preferring for the sake of convenience to pass swiftly by those which have just as many treasures to offer, but which would take longer to reach (in Venice, all distances are measured in terms of minutes and hours). These remain the preserve of the dedicated connoisseurs, specialist academics or devoted pilgrims. Important buildings such as Santa Maria Domini, for example, one of the finest constructions of the early Renaissance, or the baroque Gesuiti, an incunabulum of highly elaborate decoration, are worthy of much more than a fleeting visit yet remain at best just names for most *foresti,* or strangers. Venice, with its almost surreal atmosphere, captures the imaginations of even the most disillusioned, encouraging visitors to pluck up their courage and peep timidly around the half-open door of a palazzo, retreating quickly but not before possibly just catching a glimpse of a *felze,* the distinctive cover used on ancient gondolas, lying in the silent hall beside an elegant seventeenth-century well next to the wall. At dusk we might climb aboard the vaporetto that ploughs slowly up and down the Grand Canal, only to be further astounded by the succession of carved marble façades lit up on every side. Finally through the ogival polyphorea, the great spaces of the *porteghi,* the lowered windows of the mezzanine floors, we will be able to see the foreshortened interiors of the upper floors of those uninterrupted rows of buildings whose imposing or ethereal elevations we had only glimped hitherto. We are now able to distinguish between eras and styles within what had always been a generalized conception of the Venetian, which went hand in hand with the stereotyped image of the lagoon implanted in our collective subconscious by lessons at school, music, photographs and writings. We finally manage to harness our first impressions, which seemed like fragments of postcards, chopped out of their rightful context and pieced together in an ideal, abstract geographical place, and weave them into the one single inebriating, complex and infinitely knotted tapestry that we eventually perceive Venice to be. As the boat makes one of its stops, we look up at the brightly lit quadriphora of a magnificent palace whose name we cannot ascertain—all around us are foreigners—we are almost stupefied as we try to take in the sight of a vault illuminated by vibrant beams of light, imprisoned behind the flamboyant ogival arches of a balcony. In the center, a fresco is held aloft by elegant stucco volutes; we realize that the light is coming from below, from the walls, but even by leaning over the rail we can only see part of that brightly lit and vibrant ceiling whose shimmering and rather oneiric magnitude rapidly and quite naturally appears to be at harmony with the uneven acquatic context that we feel we are gradually beginning to understand. We are now able to realize that the various structural shapes that make up Venice can be perceived as the precious wrappings of the parallel worlds they contain. Unlike a great many other cities, where the architecture exists in its own right and the extraordinary works of art it houses are capable of autonomous life without any loss of value, here everything is consequential and irrevocably bound together. Like past Venices contained but not concealed within the closely connected buildings and forming a homonymous macrocosm, and in spite of having been furnished and decorated in periods other than that of their external shells, the reception rooms, *porteghi*, living rooms and bedrooms all reflect the same communal identity that makes this fragmented yet concentrated geographical and cultural space unique.

There have been countless literary works dedicated to the many and varied aspects of the Venetian world: the praises of this proud and exceptional people have been justly sung, in Petrarch's *Epistles* for example, and in the diaries and *carnets de voyage* of foreigners who have sojourned there throughout the centuries. During the first few centuries of the modern age, Venice was generally described as being predominantly commercial, but from the eighteenth century onwards she became known as an extraordinarily civilized place. President De Brosses, Goethe and Chateaubriand, let alone the great nineteenth-century intellectuals, all judged her to be their ideal and sentimental home, as did Byron and Ruskin with *The Stones of Venice*, to mention but a few of the most renowned. They were all gripped by the romantic image emanating from the Gothic fantasies that their collective imagination rendered so famous.

During the second half of the last century, the "tenth muse" began to transmit pictures of Venice to the rest of the world, its remains seemingly immortalized in the same clearly defined, almost crystalline evocative vistas that transported the young Proust in *La Fugitive*. Courtyard scenes were also shown where, against the background of a ruined house, working-class women could be seen drawing water from a sixteenth-century well head, possibly recording the final moments before Venice became historicized, when the city was still in step with ordinary daily life. At around this time the contemporary specialist literary works of Francesco Zanotto, Jacopo Fontana the Younger and Giuseppe Tassini were published, now indispensable seminal works of historical and artistic reference for this extraordinary *milieu* that literally overflowed with culture.

This book seeks to span the great era of architectural and artistic production from the eleventh century to the present day, in an attempt to identify the best of what is left within those precious caskets, all too often known only from the outside and sometimes either difficult or downright impossible to penetrate. We have chosen to identify spaces, lines of vision or details of interiors which, despite being contained within buildings bursting with artistic treasures that tend to monopolize the public interest, run the risk of being either forgotten or overlooked, regardless of their importance or the fascination they impart. The *Crypt of Saint Mark*, secret heart of the Basilica di San Marco, and the fine wooden roof of the church of *Santo Stefano*, an extraordinary masterpiece of invention and creative workmanship, are cases in point. Buildings like the *Scuola Levantina* and the *Palazzo Loredan* are other examples: all too often ignored because of the eccentricity of their logistics or their lack of notoriety, they are of very real interest. Thanks to the generosity of distinguished and discreet owners, we have been permitted to enter fascinating private homes within prestigious buildings which, with their furnishings and artistic treasures, collected over the centuries or acquired and put together with great enthusiasm over the last few years, have a great part to play in the discovery of Venice's interior heritage, which has hitherto largely remained either secret or spoiled.

As regards the first centuries covered by this book, religious edifices only are featured, because we could find no lay buildings or housing with contemporary furnishings or fittings. There are still those extraordinary examples of Veneto-Byzantine architecture: the *Cattedrale di Santa Maria Assunta a Torcello* and the *Basilica di Santi Maria e Donato a Murano* which appear at the beginning of the book, rightly within the Venetian context, given that they are the only buildings still retaining their basic interior scheme and typology, developed between the year 1000 and the thirteenth century, common to all the early architecture around the lagoon.

The Middle Ages made an indelible mark on Venice, imbuing her with many of the characteristics that endured resolutely throughout successive centuries. The most meaningful examples of the original essence of the Middle Ages emanated from a warrior-like and mercantile spirit that in turn owed much to the Venetians' cherished oriental roots, and responded perfectly to those patriotic and domestic virtues that formed the basis of public and private life throughout the territories, bringing life to monuments of immense and intense beauty like the Basilica di San Marco ". . . giving . . .wherever the freshness of this colouring has been preserved, the appearance of having been built of a soft and malleable substance like the wax in a giant honeycomb, and, where time has shrivelled and hardened the material and artists have embellished it with gold tracery, of being the precious binding, in the finest Cordoba leather, of the colossal Gospel of Venice." (Marcel Proust, *A la recherche du temps perdu*, *La Fugitive*—trans. C.K. Scott Moncrieff and Terence Kilmartin; and by Andreas Mayor, Chatto & Windus 1981).

The deep incisiveness of the flamboyant Gothic period, which lingered on into the sixteenth century, conferred that airy and unique *facies* on the city, leaving the hallmark of its intricate marble tracery on many of the buildings and conventual temples. Among the most famous of these are the *Palazzo Ducale* (the interior of which was completely reworked several times and which has sixteenth- and eighteenth-century additions) and the imposing building of *Santa Maria Gloriosa dei Frari*. This was the period that witnessed the building of fabulous palazzi destined for simultaneous residential and commercial use, whose traditional internal plan was codified, remaining conceptually valid for later buildings. The most significant example of this is at the *Palazzo Pesaro degli Orfei*.

The fertile and polymorphous season of the Renaissance blossomed late around the lagoon, without completely suppressing the Venetians' innate need for rich decoration, firmly rooted in the opulence of their artistry, their lines and colors, which were in fact at odds with the balanced, musical simplicity of surfaces and proportions advocated by the real founder of the Renaissance, Leon Battista Alberti. Highly skilled sculptors like Pietro Lombardo, architects like Antonio Rizzo and the Bergamasque Mauro Codussi's oeuvre was a blend of central Italic elements and flowing curvilinear Gothic traditions, emphasizing the latter's influence on the city. Mauro Codussi's masterpiece, the *Palazzo Corner Spinelli* was owned by Zuanne Corner, a friend of Michele Sanmicheli and Giorgio Vasari's Venetian patron, and became a center for fertile cultural debate.

The sixteenth century saw Venice at the height of its glory. Giorgione was the first of the legendary great sixteenth-century artists, his sensitivity to the relationship between shape and color finally overcoming the "dry, crude and stiff" approach (as Vasari puts it) learned at the Bellini workshop. He was followed by Titian with his immense production of paintings, who was Painter to the Republic for most of the century. Along with his contemporaries, Veronese and Tintoretto, Titian's work adorns many of Palladio's and Jacopo Sansovino's imposing architectural creations. Sansovino's classical style is at its finest with the design of the commemorative *Libreria di San Marco*, which was a symbol of the cultural prestige of the Republic and scene of lofty formal debate. The *Scuola Grande di San Rocco* with its suberb cycle of mannerist works by Tintoretto should not be overlooked, nor should Palladio's masterpiece, the *Basilica del Redentore*, but we wanted to draw attention to the complex and multifaceted Venetian semantic climate of the time, pointing out such diverse spaces as the *Palazzo Contarini delle Figure*, a supreme example of contrasting styles and ideas and the *Palazzo Giustinian-Recanati*, open for the first time, with its august lofty internal spaces and the splendid furnishings that successive patriotic generations have preserved intact.

The baroque style came into its own during the following century, and Venetian architecture was dominated by the work of Baldassarre Longhena. Longhena was trained under Scamozzi but managed to shrug off both his influence and the imperious dictates of Palladio, whose successors continued to observe his principles well into the eighteenth century—note Giorgio Masari's classical and luminous *Chiesa dei Gesuati*—and he managed to achieve a perfect balance between the solid mass of the buildings, the chiaroscuro of the moldings and the sumptuous opulence of the decor. Thus the scenic effects found in all forms of Venetian art became predominant, forsaking the excesses of a Roman baroque vocabulary so popular in other parts of Italy which nevertheless flourished in the interiors of buildings, with Abbondio Stazio's stucco reliefs and Andrea Brustolon's fine wood carvings. The tremendous *Chiesa della Salute* with its octagonal plan and the rooms of the *Scuola Grande dei Carmini* are examples of this; so indeed are less famous buildings like the *Scuola Levantina* synagogue, hidden away yet filled with treasures, or the *Antica Farmacia a Santa Fosca,* a fascinating old pharmacy located in the Strada Nova where the wooden scutchings after Brustolon are still in use, bearing out the fact that art was always irrevocably linked with the everyday life of the populus, themselves accustomed to beautiful and sumptuous things; indeed rich patrician patrons had their walls decorated with illusionistic paintings for their own glorification, as can be seen in the extravagant ballroom at the *Ca' Zenobio* which literally bristles with white and gold stucco work.

A hundred or so years later, during the eighteenth century, the century of Venetian rococo, Venice was again at the forefront of Italian art, although regrettably this coincided with Italy's political and economic decline. The aristocracy, mawkishly elegant, whose main purpose in life seemed to be enjoying themselves and giving masked balls, were jaded and inclined to pour huge sums of money into surrounding their houses with merrymaking; nevertheless their sublime yet disquieting world of lacquers, blown glass, fabrics, china, stucco work, canvases reflected in the glasses of a thousand mirrors has become the stuff of fairy tales, along with the frescoes that weigh down the ceilings in a perennial, stately theatrical production. The interiors of religious buildings such as the *Chiesa della Pietà* and the church of the *Gesuiti* glow with the works of Tiepolo and Giambattista Piazzetta, but we felt it well worth including other more eccentric buildings with a charm all their own, such as the *Biblioteca di San Lazzaro degli Armeni*, a library full of literary and oriental reminders. We have given considerable space to the noble palaces that were erected during the fabulous era that opened with the baroque and closed with the neoclassical. We have managed to gain access to some private houses, all the more fascinating because they are still lived in, thanks to the extreme kindness of owners, faithful conservators and perpetuators of aristocratic traditions. Naturally we have also included well-known palaces such as the *Palazzo Labia*, the *Palazzo Pisani della Moretta*, the *Palazzo Mocenigo* and the *Ca' Rezzonico*, with their stupendous Tiepolos and their dazzling, luminous *porteghi*. We are fortunate to be able to admire the fine furnishings of the *Palazzo Grimani*, the domestic luxury of the *Palazzetto Pisani* and the *Palazzo Minotto-Barbarigo*, pearls of rarified atmospheres, and the fabulous rococo mezzanine of the *Palazzo Barbarigo*—never before published—full of the works of Pietro Longhi who, along with Carlo Goldoni, was possibly the greatest cantor of the late Venetian Republican era.

The fall of the Republic, caused by Napoleon's conquest of the city in 1797, resulted in Venice becoming a French territory with Hapsburg domains on either side. By this time, the Venetians had extinguished the lights of their proud independence and the nineteenth century was greatly influenced by the stately Empire style, fine examples of which are to be found in the rooms of the then newly-erected *Ala Napoleonica* of the *Palazzo Reale*, as well as in the numerous homes which were modernized in contemporary neoclassical style such as the *Palazzo Belloni-Battagia*.

The nineteenth century was complex and difficult. It saw the redevelopment of open spaces to provide places where the cultured upper classes could meet and immerse themselves nostalgically in scutchings and furnishings belonging to a bygone age: the *Teatro della Fenice*, rebuilt several times as a result of fire, and the historic cafés in the Piazza San Marco, of which *Florian's* is the most famous, conforming to the revivalist and exotic fashion, of which the lobby of the *Danieli Hotel* is another example. The decadent, scenic interiors of the *Palazzo Pesaro degli Orfei*, created by the talented and sophisticated designer, Mariano Fortuny, are paradigmatic, glowing with the splendor of his opulent fabrics, which themselves echo the story of the Republic.

This book would not be complete without an extensive look at all the achievements of the last century. The contemporary is in fact hard to reconcile with the general idea of Venice, but many remarkable modern works coexist quite happily with the rest of her great cultural heritage. The impact of international influences has been keenly felt in twentieth-century Venice, with the famous *Hotel Excelsior* at the Lido and the legendary *Harry's Bar*. The leading postwar architect and decorator Carlo Scarpa was an outstanding master of building technique: his treatment of the *Casa Mainella* and the *Negozio Olivetti* in the Procuratie Vecchie was superlative, as was his redesigning of part of the *Palazzo Querini Stampalia*.

The book closes with a few of the exquisite and sophisticated interiors executed during the last few years, such as the *Palazzo Albrizzi* and the *Casa Pinto*, which demonstrate that the decorative traditions of this unique city are far from extinct, calling to mind the words of Gabriele d'Annunzio's protagonist in *Fuoco* on the subject of Venice, which continues to be "always a city of Life. The ideal creatures that its silence guards live throughout its past and throughout its future."

Roberto De Feo

BYZANTINE
TO FLAMBOYANT GOTHIC

Venice began to consolidate her maritime empire during the Middle Ages. Natural successor to the power of Ravenna, once the exarchate ruler of the Adriatic, Venice adopted its artistic vocabulary, the Byzantine *verbum* that has remained central to Venetian culture almost to this day.

Both the extraordinary artistic history of the churches on the island of Torcello, now deserted metaphysically speaking though densely populated during the ninth and tenth centuries, and the Basilica di San Marco, symbol of the *urbs*, proudly arrayed in marble and sparkling mosaics, bear witness to the Venetians' lust for power and to a complex and conscious reversion to their Roman roots.

The elongated typically Veneto-Byzantine arch began to appear on façades and portals throughout the city; warehouses began to be erected and the first austere dwellings of the merchant classes started to go up, all destined for further, Gothic, elaboration. The tracery window, a real challenge to the laws of statics, with its incredibly intricate interweaving of lines, arches and volutes, imbued the Palazzo Ducale and the Ca' d'Oro with that particular quality of lightness and incorporeity that is the hallmark of the Venetian flamboyant Gothic style. Generations of remarkable craftsmen from the De Sanctis, Bon, Delle Masegne and Raverti families worked the stone as tirelessly as if it had been gold.

The gigantic edifices of San Zanipolo and Santa Maria Gloriosa dei Frari began to take shape, whilst the Venetian house assumed its definitive form. The *portego*, a long hall, ran the full depth of those houses destined for domestic use, erupting onto the façade in an airy and elegant polyphora. Above this were smaller rooms, the *amezzàdi*, often opening off each other. This building tradition continued, largely unchanged, throughout the life of the Venetian Republic.

It was during this period, which lasted until the Renaissance, that the city began to grow. It was a lively and constructive time, restless, feverish, subject to countless different influences, inspired by Moorish art.

The adventurous journeyings of the Polo family, the river of gold, pearls, silk, spices and perfumes that poured inexorably from the East in those days, the Sack of Constantinople in 1204 and the capture of Saint Mark's body in Alexandria, all played their part in the quite unprecedented bellicose yet supremely mercantile early Republican era, so beautifully described in John Ruskin's celebrated book, *The Stones of Venice*.

Cupolas of the Basilica di San Marco

Cattedrale di Santa Maria Assunta a Torcello

The Island of Torcello is a place of surreal silence and solitude, as if its palaces, houses and convents have been engulfed by the lagoon. The island conserves some magnificent testaments to its past, such as the Chiesa di Santa Fosca and Santa Maria Assunta, the cathedral founded in 639 by Isacio, Byzantine exarch, or governor of Ravenna under Emperor Heraclius, rebuilt in the eleventh century as a Byzantine basilica. The severe and evocative interior, with its rich polychrome marble, gold mosaics, and sumptuous pavement, shimmers in the pure and magical light of the island. The nave is separated from the aisles by simplified Corinthian columns which support semicircular arches. The chancel is bounded by an early eleventh-century iconostasis, composed of six columns, interspersed with four marble plutei with sculpted reliefs of animals and plant motifs in a refined Byzantine style. The columns support a series of fifteenth-century paintings on wood with gold backgrounds, above which rises a large, majestic wooden crucifix. At the opposite end, above the main entrance, is a grandiose twelfth- or thirteenth-century mosaic of the Veneto-Byzantine school depicting the Apotheosis of Christ and the Last Judgement. The narrative elements mark a departure from the rigid hieratic style of the artistic circles of Ravenna. In the lunette, the serene representation of the madonna also testifies to this desire for formal liberty, suggesting the first Venetian glimmer of naturalism. It contrasts with the powerful image of the Virgin Mary as the *Teotoga* (the mother of God), a solitary figure of Byzantine grandeur set in majesty against an immense golden background in the conch of the apse.

BASILICA DEI SANTI MARIA E DONATO A MURANO

Originally built to venerate the Virgin, this church was later also dedicated to Saint Donatus when his body was transferred here from Cephalonia in 1152. Constructed in around 1000, soon after San Marco, Santi Maria e Donato was restored to its original appearance following restoration in the nineteenth century. This basilica has a tall transept and two aisles separated from the nave by columns of Greek marble. The ship's keel roof is typically Venetian. In the apse, dominated by a thirteenth-century Byzantine mosaic of the madonna, saints painted in fresco in the style of Giotto during the fourteenth century mount guard around the baroque altar, which is crowned by a high, elaborate tabernacle. But it is above all the superb pavement, contemporary with that of San Marco and executed in 1140, which makes the church unique. This marvelous Veneto-Byzantine mosaic combines *opus vermiculatum* using small pieces of marble and polychrome vitreous paste, and *opus sectile* using larger segments of marble. The interior design of the basilica features symbolic figures alternated with varied and imaginative ornamental motifs, such as the two colonnades with their Byzantine capitals and slender Veneto-Byzantine arcature.

CLOISTER OF SANT'APOLLONIA

A jewel of Roman architecture, this cloister is the oldest in the city. Although situated close to the crowded Piazzo San Marco, the interior has retained all its charm and mystical solitude. Peace and serenity enrapture visitors almost as soon as they have crossed the threshold. Semicircular arches of different heights and spans are supported by short columns—paired on two sides, single on the other two—which form a rhythmic sequence marking the perimeter of the cloister. The capitals are in a late Byzantine style, as is the coping of the well, whose delicate sculpted decoration make it the center around which the space flows. The cloister, originally part of a monastery founded by the Benedictines—the order which introduced Roman principles throughout Europe—dates from the first years of the eleventh century. From the fifteenth century until the fall of the Republic, the monastery was the residence of the Primicerio di San Marco, the highest ecclesiastical dignitary in the Venetian ducal chapel.

CRYPT OF THE BASILICA DI SAN MARCO

The ducal chapel and symbol of the power of the Republic, where civic and religions virtues had to coincide, the Basilica di San Marco formed a cohesive element for the first settlers in the lagoon. The Golden Basilica saw the light of day in 832, four years after the body of Saint Mark was transferred from Alexandria. The evangelist became the patron saint of the city, replacing Saint Theodore, symbol of Byzantine rule. The cathedral's oriental forms nonetheless stem from Constantinople, and were modeled on the two imperial basilicas of Hagia Sophia and Holy Apostles. The Republic enriched the edifice with priceless works of art and treasures. Adorned with royal porphyry, mosaics, and polychrome marbles, San Marco is an astonishing repository for the most diverse languages and cultures. The façade is crowned by the famous horses which once adorned the hippodrome in Constantinople,

as if to symbolize the city's emancipation from, and superiority over, an exhausted eastern empire. The celebrated basilica still contains some little-known, unfrequented areas, including the powerfully built crypt where Saint Mark's body was buried in 1094. Brick ribbed vaults supported by short columns of luminous Greek marble with Byzantine capitals animate this austere, simple space. A marble screen decorated with graceful religious motifs delineates the central area where the altar stands, crowned by a late fifteenth-century marble relief, behind which the remains of the saint were found during restoration in 1811. Certain panaches of the vault feature vestiges of early fifteenth-century frescoes, including a severe Saint Anthony standing under a simplified ogival arch. In the late sixteenth century, the crypt was flooded and abandoned; it was only opened for worship in 1889.

Palazzo Ducale

The doges' palace, seat of the Republican government and the highest magistrates of the state, the law court, public record office, armory, and prison, the Palazzo Ducale was all of these at once. This enormous building—the only one in the city which merited being called a palace, distinguishing it from the houses of the nobility known as Ca' (casa)—was the theater of the most important and significant episodes in the history of Venice, a witness to the glorious and tragic vicissitudes of the secular grandeur of the Serenissima. It was built successively in Byzantine, Gothic, and Renaissance style, but it is the latter two which characterize the splendid architecture seen today. In addition to its political and administrative functions, the Palazzo also housed a marvelous collection of works of art glorifying the Republic. The frescoes of Veronese, Tintoretto, Palma the Younger, Jacopo da Ponte, and Titian, as well as the sculptures of Sansovino, Tiziano Aspetti, Campagna, Alessandro Vittoria illustrate the institutions and military victories of the Serenissima. The Scala d'Oro (golden staircase), whose vaulted ceiling is decorated with late sixteenth-century stuccoes by Alessandro Vittoria, evokes the power of the doges, who exploited every opportunity to flaunt their political and economic supremacy. As in the grand staircase of the Libreria Sansoviniana (Sansovinian Library), also known as the Libreria Marciana,

there are, between the stout ribs of the vaults, allegorical frescoes by Battista Franco framed by stuccoes which have a mannerist flavor. In contrast, the candelabra on the pilasters and the extrados of the arches are Renaissance in style. Their ornamental motif is taken from the classical Roman repertoire, adopted by Raphael and his school, which one finds in the bas-reliefs and the grotesques sculpted by Giovanni da Udine for the Palazzo Grimani at Santa Maria Formosa. If the Scala d'Oro illustrates the role of the doge's residence in official state ceremony, the Chancellery, once filled with the noisy and feverish activity of a crowd of bureaucrats employed in drafting and tabulating the acts of state or secret documents of the highest magistrates of the Republic, testifies to the Palazzo's administrative importance. The ceiling, with its massive framework of beams, has a skylight which opens onto the roof and serves to light the hall. The sixteenth-century furnishings are original: on either side of the hall two long symmetrical rows of cupboards are linked by a graceful balustrade with a small central gate. The upper parts of the cupboard doors feature the emblems of all the various chancellors since 1268, together with their names and the dates they took office. At opposite ends of the hall are two large desks, still in their original positions, behind which the head secretary and the Vice-regent used to sit.

Chiesa di Santo Stefano

This Gothic church, dedicated to Saint Stephen the first Christian martyr, was built in the thirteenth century as an Augustinian monastic church, totally rebuilt in the fourteenth and then transformed in a flamboyant Gothic style in the fifteenth century. The interior consists of three tall naves, separated by fourteenth-century columns with rich polychrome and gilded capitals which support ogival arches. The brick masonry is decorated with beautiful repeated plant motifs in a refined Gothic style. In the aisles, superb baroque altars, enriched with precious marbles, alternate with funerary monuments, including that of Francesco Morosini, known as

the Peloponnesian, one of the great doges of Venice, buried at Santo Stefano in 1694. Situated in the main nave, it was made by Filippo Parodi. Behind the majestic marble high altar crowned by a tall typanum, light enters the monk's choir through large windows in the polygonal apse. Lit on either side by a row of semicircular windows, the imposing ship's keel roof is ornamented with a highly detailed coffered ceiling decorated with a repeated rosette motif. This superb piece of fifteenth-century carpentry echoes the secular experience of the master craftsmen who worked in the shipyards of the Arsenale and whose influence extended throughout Europe.

CHIESA DI SANTA MARIA GLORIOSA DEI FRARI

Founded by the *frari*, the minor friars of Saint Francis whose presence in the lagoon dates from 1222, this immense Gothic church used to be known as the Ca' Grande. Reconstruction began in 1340 and was completed towards the middle of the fifteenth century. In its spatial configuration and architectural style, this grandiose brick structure is in many ways similar to the neighboring Chiesa di Santi Giovanni e Paolo, with which, moreover, it shares the role of pantheon of Republican glories. Santa Maria Gloriosa dei Frari is a veritable monument to that austere religious fervor which, according to John Ruskin, was responsible for Venice's superiority over other cities. The vast interior consists of a tall nave separated from two aisles by twelve thick columns and culminating in a luminous choir, where the majestic *Assumption* by Titian stands out against the splendid ogival bays of the apse. The gigantic Gothic vault has intersecting ribs combined with a vibrant succession of larger transverse ribs in a geometric repetition that recalls the structure of a canon from the timid fifteenth-century beginnings of Flemish polyphonic music, and which draws the eye along the nave, giving this extraordinary interior a strong longitudinal emphasis. The *catene*, wooden tie beams whose purpose is to reinforce the frame of the building, are characteristic of traditional local construction methods and punctuate the restless, abstract Gothic vault, which contrasts with the religious serenity of the Renaissance *Calvary*, dominated by the large crucifix above the arch leading into the monks' choir. Built in 1475, this choir is today the only one in Venice still in its original position in the middle of the nave, the area that used to be reserved for monastic ceremonies. The high marble screen surrounding the choir, probably by the Bons workshop, has flamboyant Gothic stylistic features combined with the Renaissance vocabulary of the Lombardi, who completed the choir in the last quarter of the fifteenth century.

The stalls consist of 124 seats divided into three rows and are the work of Marco Cozzi, who completed them in 1468. Each seat is decorated with a marquetry landscape and a sculpted relief of a saint, dominated by a large, richly ornamented shell. The arrows at the top of the decoration are clearly Gothic in style. The Humanist inspiration of these stalls contrasts with certain late, nostalgic, northern influences. The juxtaposition of these two tendencies is the reason for the complexity of these stalls, and provides us with a key to the historical and artistic interpretation of this majestic church.

RENAISSANCE AND MANNERISM

Venice and the Renaissance: two antithethical concepts, not easy to reconcile. At the beginning of the sixteenth century, the Serenissima—as Venice was known—having feared for her life after the aggression of the League of Cambrai and the defeat of Agnadello, closed in on herself, impervious to the new Humanistic ideas emanating from central Italy. In fact it took until Sansovino's arrival after the Sack of Rome in 1527 for the Renaissance to take root in Venice. Jacopo Sansovino was its first architect, in the modern sense of the word, and his arrival heralded a new, intense season of architectural vitality.

Venice fell under the spell of the Renaissance considerably later than the Sforza city of Milan and the great Humanist cities of Florence, Rome and nearby Padua where Donatello had so powerfully influenced Squarcione and in turn Mantegna.

Parts of the city became workshops for the new architectural ideas: the Rialto market, pulsating heart of commerce, rebuilt by Scarpagnino after the terrible fire of 1514; the Arsenale, a veritable hotbed of production; the area around San Francesco della Vigna where the doge Andrea Vitti set Jacopo Sansovino the task of proving his worth as an architect before letting him loose on the mammoth challenge of the Piazza San Marco.

The fantastic architectural Venetian Renaissance closed with Palladio's famous reordering of the island of San Giorgio Maggiore, which provided a marvelous counterattraction to the *mise-en-scène* of San Marco. There was a heady and diverse mixture of artistic vocabularies: Lombardo revived the elements of local tradition, the Palazzo Zen is a fine example of oriental influences, and there is the lofty classicism and harmonious proportions of Sanmicheli and Palladio. This was a chiaroscuro yet sumptuous time for Venice, and heralded an era of unparallelled cultural and worldly splendor unaffected by the fact that its watery dominion was being steadily eroded by the advancing Turks and by the opening of the new Atlantic routes. Venice's many talented artists included Bellini, Tintoretto, Giorgione, the grandiose Veronese, and the mighty Titian. It was a time of unprecedented and ostentatious splendor that flaunted the Sumptuary laws introduced in a futile attempt to curb the Venetians' insatiable desire for luxury, and they were proud of their city's appellative of "Queen of the Adriatic."

Venice saw itself as the third Rome, heir to the power of Constantinople, a center of philosophical studies and musical innovation. The Flemish composer Adrian Willaert became *maestro di cappella* at the Basilica di San Marco, where his tradition of grand church music was amplified by Andrea and Giovanni Gabrieli and later, at the beginning of the seventeenth century, by the celebrated composer Monteverdi.

The Porta dell'Arsenale

PALAZZO CORNER SPINELLI-RUBELLI

This palace, typical of the architecture of Mauro Cordussi, who attempted to integrate new developments taking place in central Italy into the local tradition, is one of the most original early Renaissance buildings in Venice. According to Giorgio Vasari, the interior was transformed in 1542 by Michele Sanmicheli, a good friend of the master of the house, Giovanni Corner. The beautiful marble fireplace, sculpted in the sixteenth century, is supported by two dramatic telamons, forming a striking counterpoint to the serene, precise calligraphy of the graceful mantelpiece decoration, interspersed with fine triglyphs. Mannerism, however, triumphs once again with the grotesque masks, their streaming ribbons twisting like snakes, which contrast with the garland of fruit below. This refined, complex work has been attributed to Jacopo Sansovino, who settled in Venice in 1527 following the Sack of Rome. The baroque bust above the fireplace is probably a portrait of Giovanni II Corner, who was doge of Venice from 1709 to 1722.

PALAZZO CONTARINI DELLE FIGURE

Andrea Palladio was a frequent visitor to this palace, famous for its library and the remarkable collection of paintings assembled in the sixteenth century by Jacopo Contarini, a friend and patron of the great architect. The decoration in the dining room, which dates from that period, includes a monumental fireplace dominated by a large frieze depicting scenes from mythology punctuated with gold mannerist cartouches. The fireplace is decorated with alternating bucranes, small panoplies and patera, separated by triglyphs. On the mantelpiece rest two white and gold classical figures supporting a shell which serves as a background for a Roman bust. This superb piece of stucco modeling from the school of Alessandro Vittoria echoes the extraordinary work of Primaticcio at the Château of Fontainebleau. The ceiling, which dates from the end of the sixteenth century, is decorated *alla sansovina*, densely ornamented with small mannerist cartouches, stylized scrolls and rosettes in contrasting tonalities. The vivid scarlet of the walls—the color was selected by the current owner, Pierluigi Pizzi, the internationally renowned cinematographer and director—add to the room's theatrical atmosphere.

Chiesa di Santa Maria Mater Domini

The Renaissance church, situated on the square of the same name, is hidden among older buildings, including the thirteenth-century Case Zane, with its rare Veneto-Byzantine loggia, and the pre-Gothic Palazzo Barbaro e Viaro. Built on a Greek cross plan, the church has tall stone columns and cornices which create an elegant counterpoint to the white plaster. The cupola above the transept is reminiscent of the central cupola of San Marco and interracts harmoniously with a space defined by spare architectural forms which recall Tuscan architecture. Above the high altar is a relief in colored stucco depicting the Virgin and Child; this relief, in the style of Donatello, is further evidence of the strong impact of Tuscan Renaissance art and architecture on a fiercely Gothic Venice, thanks chiefly to the work of Sansovino. In the right arm of the transept, *The Last Supper* by Bonifacio dei Pitati forms a pendant to the *Invention of the Cross* by Tintoretto on the opposite wall; below this brilliant work is a Veneto-Byzantine bas-relief in gilded marble of the Virgin, for whom the church is named.

SCUOLA GRANDE DI SAN ROCCO

According to Venetian tradition, on 16 August, the feast day of Saint Roch, the Campo San Rocco became the venue for a formal celebration attended by the doge and the *signoria*. Beginning in the seventeenth century, the square also became a place where painters could exhibit their work, similar to the contemporary exhibitions of paintings in Rome at San Salvatore in Lauro. This vast Renaissance building was the headquarters of the Scuola di San Rocco, a confraternity founded in 1478. Construction was begun under the direction of Bartolomeo Bon in 1515 and completed under Sante Lombardo and Scarpagnino between 1527 and 1549. Tintoretto painted a celebrated sequence of fifty-two paintings for the confraternity, including a series depicting episodes from the Old Testament for the ceiling of the Sala Grande (the main upper hall). These magnificent compositions, with their impassioned chiaroscuro, are framed by gilded wood reliefs in a late mannerist style. The paintings of scenes from the New Testament are also by Tintoretto, as is the retable of the high altar. Magnificent carvings running completely around the walls of this large hall enhance the rich colors of the paintings. Large procession lanterns, which date from the eighteenth century, contrast with the dark panelling and the beautiful polychrome marble pavement, relaid at the end of the nineteenth century. The Sala Grande of the Scuola di San Rocco houses other paintings, such as the *Annunciation* by Titian and two works by Giambattista Tiepolo, *Abraham Visited by an Angel* and *Hagar and Ishmael Comforted by an Angel* painted in 1732, which show that the young artist had already freed himself from the influence of his former teacher, Giambattista Piazzetta.

LIBRERIA DI SAN MARCO

Constructed between 1537 and 1554 by Jacopo Sansovino, this superb edifice testifies to sixteenth-century Venice's determination assume the role of heir to the Byzantine Empire following its fall in 1453. Indeed, many of the codices offered to the Republic in 1468 by Cardinal Bessarione, an ardent defender of Humanism and ecumenicism, came from Constantinople. His bequest formed the basis of the library and included the celebrated fifteenth-century *Grimani Breviary* as well as works by Aldo Manuzio, among them the *Hypnerotomachia Poliphili*, which played a major role in forming the Renaissance imagination. On either side of the main entrance are two colossal mannerist caryatids, sculpted by Alessandro Vittoria in 1553–1555 with the help of Lorenzo Rubini. The vault above the sumptuous staircase features a geometrical structure of octagons and squares adorned with allegorical stucco figures, paintings by Giovan Battista Franco and Battista del Moro, as well as grotesques and gilding. The Vestibolo (hall), intended to house the school of philosophy and rhetoric, assumed its present appearence in 1597 when it was totally transformed by Vincenzo Scamozzi. This grand and austere hall further illustrates the influence of Rome on the Serenissima. The light entering through the large bays is reflected by the polished surface of the pavement, a veritable marquetry of polychrome marble arranged in a design of concentric circles. The niches with their Ionic columns crowned by typana and the projecting cornice which interrupts the Corinthian pilasters at mid-height were designed to display the rich archaeological collections bequeathed to the Republic by Cardinal Domenico Grimani and his grandson Giovanni, patriarch of Aquileia. The spectacular late mannerist ceiling is adorned with a series of trompe l'oeil columns in golden brown tones by the painters Cristoforo and Stefano Rosa from Brescia and took a decade to paint, from 1550 to 1560. In the center, the magisterial *Wisdom* by Titian symbolizes the library's function.

PALAZZO GIUSTINIAN-RECANATI

One of the last large patrician residences still inhabited, this vast palace was originally built for the Trevisan family. The simple, robust exterior gives no hint of the riches inside. The Giustinians, a family always divided into several branches, is one of the four great Venetian patrician families who signed the act founding the Serenissima in 725 and who enjoyed a hereditary title. Of the innumerable personalities who contributed to the glory of this family, several deserve mention: San Lorenzo Giustinian, first patriarch of Venice, Marcantonio Giustinian, the commander-in-chief of the army who became doge in 1684, and Giacomo, tireless defender of the Republic against Napoleon. The interior of the palace obeys the conventions of the sixteenth century, both in terms of overall design and the decoration of the rooms, where high, austere wooden ceilings are decorated *alla sansovina*. The sumptuous red salon, so-named because of the scarlet brocade fabric on the walls, echoed by the darker tones of the large oriental carpet, provides a perfect setting for the exceptional sixteenth-century paintings; the masterpiece of this collection is the large canvas by Tintoretto depicting, in dense and dramatic chiaroscuro, the departure of Caterina Cornaro for her ill-fated marriage with the king of Cyprus. The eagle of Byzance appears in various places in this palace, which was inhabited without interruption by the Giustinian family, a reminder that they can trace their ancestry back to the emperor Justinian.

Basilica del Redentore

One of the most renowned basilicas in Venice, the Basilica del Redentore was built, in accordance with the wishes of the Senate, to celebrate the end of the great plague of 1576. The design was entrusted to one of the great figures of Venetian architecture, Andrea Palladio. The interior, in the form of a Latin cross, combines two types of design, basilican and centrally planned, in order to fulfill different liturgical demands. In the aisles, three ajacent chapels are separated by coupled Corinthian engaged columns. The isolated high altar, which has an imposing tabernacle decorated with bronzes, is by the artist Giuseppe Mazza, a native of Bologna. Mazza's altar remplaced the original, more modest one with statues of Saint Mark, Saint Francis and a bronze Christ, all by Gerolamo Campagna, which were incorporated into the new altar. The barrel vault is interrupted by large bays which create beautiful effects of light. Each year, on the third Sunday in July, this famous church is decorated with sumptuous brocades and damasks for the Festa del Redentore. Venetians reach the church by crossing the canal from La Giudecca via a bridge of boats, reviving the traditional procession which, until the fall of the Republic, commemorated the senate's resolution and in which the doge and the highest dignitaries of the state participated.

Chiesa di San Salvador

The interior of this church is a perfect illustration of Venetian high Renaissance architecture. Thanks to the three lanterns that Vincenzo Scamozzi added to the cupolas in 1569, the interior is bathed in light. The polychrome marble pavement follows the architectural plan in a multitude of geometrical forms, stopping at the high altar, which features the glowing *Transfiguration* by Titian. Another masterpiece by the same artist, a late work depicting the Annunciation, adorns the Capella Cornovi.
On the high altar, dominating the whole of this enormous space, is a sculpture of the Savior, holding the standard which symbolizes salvation, the triumph over death.
The *Transfiguration* by Titian conceals the famous *Pala d'Oro*, a masterpiece of Venetian Gothic gold plate, which is solemnly displayed to the public only once a year, on the feast day of the church's patron saint.

THE BAROQUE ERA

Compared with the previous or indeed the following centuries, the Venetian Seicento is at a definite disadvantage. The Republic's position of preeminence over the Mediterranean declined steadily during the course of the seventeenth century, in spite of the victory at the Battle of Lepanto in 1572. England and Holland, however, the latest stars in the mercantile firmament, proudly led the way to America where fantastic riches were to be won. Thanks to the theologian Paolo Sarpi's skillful defence, the city managed to wrest its political autonomy and its sovereignty back from the hands of the Pope, who had placed it under an interdict. Under these circumstances, it is hardly surprising that the great baroque tide flowing up from Rome, and the singular achievements of Bernini and Borromini, those great pioneers of the triumphal Counter-Reformation, scarcely touched Venice. The architectural scene around Venice was dominated by a single great man: Baldassarre Longhena. His greatest achievement was the imposing articulated mass of the Basilica di Santa Maria della Salute, a spectacular building with a central plan, the rhythm of the traditional tripartite façade of the Venetian palazzo altered by the introduction of a powerful sequence of continuous windows.

Towards the end of the century, extraordinary stucco reliefs began to appear on ceilings and on walls, primarily the work of Tencalla. The exceptional and inspired woodcarver Andrea Brustolon, trained by the Genovese Parodi, created outstanding sculptural furniture. He produced armchairs and *consolles*, theatrically supported by exotically clad Moorish figures, *potiches* for the East India Company, silver and *vermeil* for rich displays of tableware, all of which graced increasingly fashionable drawing rooms. Lace from Burano and the marvelous glass from Murano so enchanted the rest of Europe that Colbert, Louis XIV's Minister of Finance, was driven first to impose crippling levies on them and then to create the modern French luxury industry.

It was a century of political crisis, but the Serenissima continued to defend its power tenaciously, glorious in its defeat of the Turks: the doge Francesco Morosini reconquered the Peloponnese in 1688. It was a complex and troubled period, a significant prelude to the final, grandiose and definitive act which was about to unfold.

Basilica di Santa Maria della Salute

Basilica di Santa Maria della Salute

Venetians make a yearly pilgrimage to Santa Maria della Salute on 21 November to commemorate the decree of 1630 which led to its construction. This sumptuous basilica, with its sculptures, gigantic Corinthian pilasters, and cupola crowned by the Virgin holding a sea captain's staff, magnificently marks the point where the Grand Canal enters the San Marco basin. The vast, solemn interior is bathed in the light that enters through sixteen large windows, which are separated into pairs by wooden statues of prophets by an unknown artist. The vertical sequence of volumes that delineates the passage from the octagonal nave to the circular area under the dome is most impressive. Corinthian engaged columns—of a type, according to Vitruvius, once used in classical temples devoted to female divinities and subsequently adopted for buildings dedicated to the Virgin—separate the arches surrounding the ambulatory, which has six apsidial chapels and adjoins the choir. The handsome neoclassical silver chandelier by Giuseppe Borsato was offered to the city in 1836. The polychrome marble flagstones are arranged in concentric circles forming a richly colored spiral. At the center is the inscription, "unde origo, inde salus" (From the Origins Came Salvation) celebrating the city's beginnings and reflecting the Venetians' traditional devotion to the Madonna, because the date of the city's founding, 25 March 421, coincides with the festival of the Annunciation. The five rose motifs in the center and the thirty-two others which adorn the first large circle, together with the stars of David, recall the Virgin Mary's genealogical kinship with the Biblical king, and are also symbols commonly associated with Marian worship.

Scuola Levantina

In 1541, the Senate granted the Levantine Jewish merchants official permission to settle in the quarter of Venice known as the *Ghetto Vecchio*. This small but influential Mediterranean community was composed of refugees fleeing the Spanish and Portuguese Inquisitions, as well as people from the various regions of the Ottoman Empire. The Scuola, which contains their synagogue, took on its present appearance following the extensive renovations ordered by the community's official council in 1680.

The interior, the most sumptuous in the old Venetian Jewish quarter, has an astonishing profusion of decoration. In keeping with the precepts of Judaism, the hall of worship is devoid of any paintings, but antique brocades cover the walls, an abundance of bronze and silver lamps hang from the ceiling, and deeply colored wood furnishings contrast spectacularly with the rich red curtains. The coffered ceiling, carved with powerful concentric frames in relief, is attributed to Andrea Brustolon. This visionary and virtuoso interpreter of the baroque in Venice probably also designed the magnificent bema, an imposing structure made of black walnut. The horseshoe staircase is lavishly carved with bas-reliefs that combine Biblical imagery with decorative elements of baroque inspiration. The two twisted columns, an allegorical allusion to the columns of Solomon's temple, frame the pulpit, lending the ensemble a grandeur reminicent of Bernini, enhanced by the evocative light that enters through the small window in the apsidiole.

FARMACIA AI DUE SAN MARCHI

Originally located on the Campo San Stin, this ancient pharmacy was reconstructed and transferred to Ca' Rezzonico in 1908. The walnut panelling and furnishings of the consulting room, including the curved rococo desk, date from the eighteenth century while a marvelous collection of 183 pharmacy jars in glazed faience from the Cozzi porcelain factory line the shelves. The simpler pine panelling of the medecine shelves is carved with pilasters, grotesque masks, and other decorative elements. The pharmacy's collection also includes seventeenth-century *albarelli*—seventy-six in all—as well as thirty beautiful small bottles made of Murano glass.

ANTICA FARMACIA A SANTA FOSCA

By the end of the sixteenth century Venice had a number of pharmacies, two of which still exist today. One is located inside the monastery of the Capuchin friars of the Redeemer, and the other, still in use, at Santa Fosca in the Strada Nova. The severe baroque interior, furnished with carved walnut pieces, is attributed to Andrea Brustolon. The ceiling *alla sansovina*, the pharmacy jars in eighteenth-century Venetian faience, the allegorical statues, and the gilded dark wood panelling imbue the interior with a unique charm.

Chiesa dei Gesuiti o di Santa Maria Assunta

Following a great deal of controversy, the members of the Jesuit order were admitted to Venice in 1657. They settled near the Fondamente Nuove—somewhat removed from the city center and still under construction—where earlier in the century the doge Leonardo Donà had decided to build a palace. The old medieval church was rebuilt in the eighteenth century by Domenico Rossi. The building, inspired by baroque architecture in Rome, has a long nave with deep chapels. This and the imposing baroque decoration are typical of Jesuit churches. Stuccoes by Abbondio Stazio enhance the two ceiling frescoes by Francesco Fontebasso. Andrea Pozzo the Elder conceived the spatial organization of the church. Imposing pillars lead up the nave towards the altar in a vigorous rhythmic sequence and are covered by sumptuous trompe l'œil marble, designed to resemble a rich brocade and inscribed with the white and green monogram of the Manin family. Wealthy patricians wishing to affirm their recently-acquired noble status, the Manin family invested an enormous amount of money in this church. The decoration culminates in a spectacular high altar clearly inspired by Bernini, supported by ten green twisted columns above which rises a tabernacle inlaid with lapis lazuli. The striking architecture, bold use of color, and theatrical quality of the abundant decoration make this church, little frequented by tourists, both a unique edifice built *ad majorem Dei gloriam* and a showcase to celebrate the importance of a patrician family.

SCUOLA GRANDE DEI CARMINI

The Scuola dei Carmini, founded to counter the anti-Marian doctrines propagated by the Protestant Reformation, was initially installed in a church of the same name before moving in 1625 to neighboring buildings converted by the architect Cantello. In 1667, Baldassare Longhena reconstructed the building on the corner of the *campo* which became the Scuola. A large staircase, decorated with baroque stuccoes by Abbondi Stazio, leads to the upper hall, which is renowned for the ceiling decoration by Giambattista Tiepolo. Commisioned in 1739 by the prior Giambattista Orlandini and inspired by Veronese's works in the Sala del Collegio at the Palazzo Ducale, the cycle occupied ten years of the painter's life. The ceiling, divided into nine compartments, is painted with an *Allegory of Virtue* and elegant angelic figures, culminating with the central scene of Saint Simon Stock receiving the scapular—a monastic vestment—from the Madonna. Tiepolo's use of color and his palette of light pastel tones imbues these works with wonderful luminosity, revealing the artist at the peak of his mature style. The expressive force of these frescoes fulfilled all the expectations of the friars, who wanted something worthy of being "displayed until the end of the world."

Ca' Zenobio

The magnificent palace near the church of Santa Maria dei Carmini was built at the end of the seventeenth century for the Zenobios—a wealthy patrician family of Greek origin—on the site of a fourteenth-century edifice belonging to the Marosini family. The architect, Antonio Gaspari, a pupil and collaborator of Longhena, was better known for interior decoration and modernization than for designing buildings. The ballroom on the *piano nobile* is the culmination of the palace's lavish decor. On the walls, stucco motifs are combined with brightly colored paintings by Dorigny, while on the ceiling the complex artifices of the *quadratura*—mythological fables, foreshortened nude figures, garlands, rich trompe l'œil oriental fabrics, and laughing putti—reflect the exuberance of the baroque universe. Large mirrors add to the magical asmosphere, creating the impression that this sumptuous salon extends to infinity. Interspersed with the allegories and the urns overflowing with flowers, as if to advertise the wealth and power of the palace's owners, is the family coat of arms. The entrance to the *portego* is dominated by the musicans' loggia, which is supported by the gilded consoles of the *serliana*. The *portego* itself is decorated with three landscapes by Luca Carlevarijs, an artist so closely identified with the Zenobio family that he was known as "Luca di Ca' Zenobio."

The other reception rooms feature lively white and gold stucco decoration. The ornate overdoors are carved with joyful putti holding sculpted gilt medallions that contain mythological scenes, such as the contest between Apollo and Marsyas. The cornices, shells, draperies, acanthus leaves and other ornamental elements are reminiscent of the Palazzo Albrizzi and suggest that these stuccoes may be the work of Abbondio Stazio, a Ticinese artist who, along with Tencalla, was one of the greatest masters of this delicate art.

THE EIGHTEENTH CENTURY

The Settecento saw the final fading rays of the Serenissma's golden decadence and with them a whole civilization. This was Venice's *grand siècle,* a cornucopia of unimaginable treasures and glories, her scintillating festivities continuing to attract powerful men and adventurers, deposed kings and intellectuals, comedians and musicians from all over Europe. The century opened with the melancholy notes of Benedetto Marcello and the Prete Rosso and the ethereal figures of Sebastiano Ricci, but was soon transported by Tiepolo's epic works. His style was delicate but solemn, full of light, impalpable yet sculptural.

No one great architect made his mark on the fabric of the city. Venice had become crystallized in the image both of its own magnitude and its Palladian grandeur and in spite of various attempts at change, she remained under a spell that, stupified and incredulous, she was only to break when her defences finally gave way under Napoleon's urgent and unstoppable onslaught. However, although the *facies urbis* remained unchanging, the interiors of the palaces, veritable treasure houses, contained the most sumptuous decorations and furnishings. Splendid stucco work, fantastic frescoes, brocaded silks, carved or laquered furniture and glittering, curiously shaped chandeliers were all reflected in an intoxicating revelry in the mirrors large and small that replicated themselves everywhere, throwing open nonexistent, never-ending rooms, spaces dreamy and far away. This was the age of the *casini,* where the most important ladies, free from the constraints of their social classes, received their friends and lovers, gossiped or made polite conversation and discussed the subversive ideas emanating from beyond the Alps; this was where huge fortunes were to be lost in a single night at the gaming tables. Masks were worn during some of the months of the year, encouraging seduction, their mystery breaking down the social barriers. This was the world of Goldoni and Longhi, with Venice fading into a black and gold sunset. The Republic seemed to want to die away leaving a legend of irretrievable atmospheres behind it: along with Naples under Charles III of Bourbon, Venice was held to be the finest musical city in Europe, and at least 1,274 productions were staged in its many theaters, while the charitable institutions became centers of non-stop artistic activity. The Serenissima welcomed her illustrious visitors, plunging them into a heady vortex of sumptuous banquets given by members of the aristocracy, all bent on outdoing each other. It was the city immortalized in Canaletto's paintings, the blue-green sea studded with precious vessels, seemingly suspended forever in a refined and timeless luminosity, but it was also the submissive and solitary city, slightly disquieting and lost, of Francesco Guardi's silent *vedute.*

Chiesa di San Stae

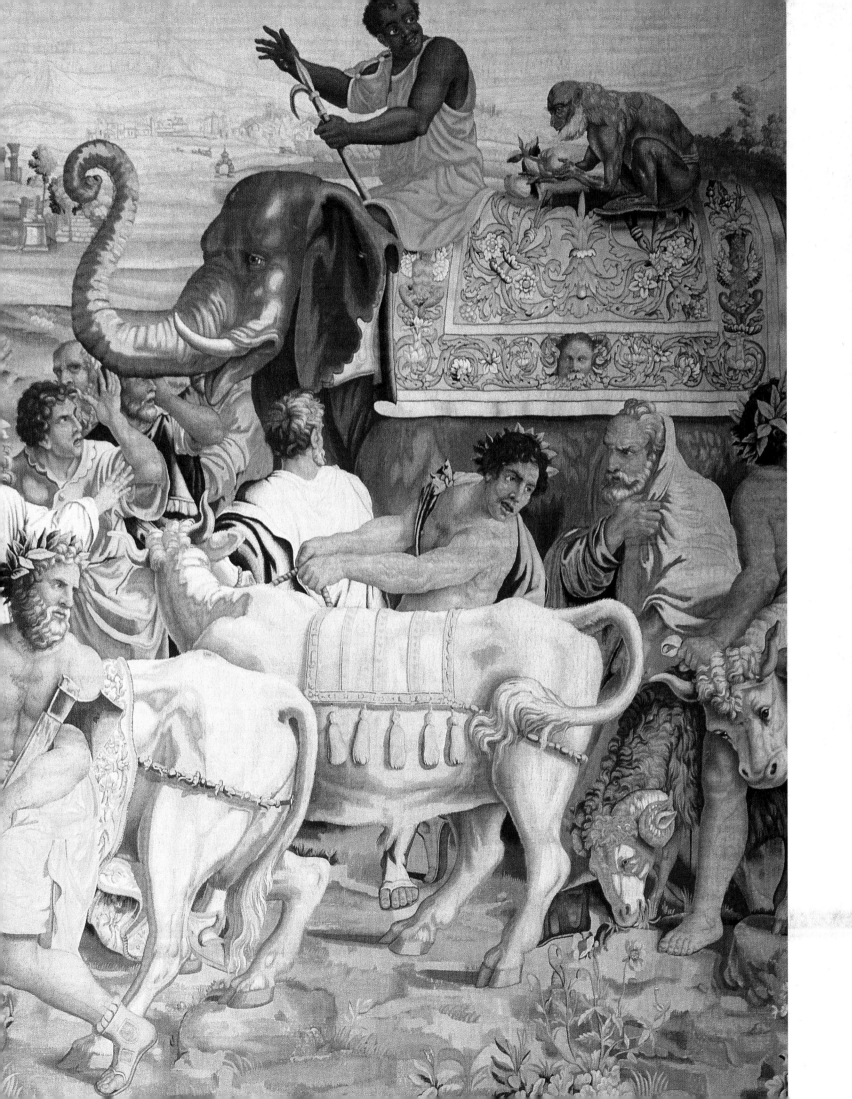

PALAZZO LABIA

Built in around 1700 for the Labias, a family of Spanish origin admitted to the Venetian patriciate in 1647, this palace crowns the great baroque era in Venice. The architecture of the massive building, located between the Grand Canal and the Rio di Cannaregio, is derived directly from Longhena. Throughout the century, the proud Labia family, determined to obscure their common origins, continually astounded the Venetian aristocracy with unprecedentedly lavish parties and receptions. The family's fabulous wealth was reflected in a ritual that took place at the conclusion of every fête: the family motto, "L'abia o non l'abia, saro sempre Labia" (with or without I will always be Labia) would be pronounced, upon which the guests would throw the precious dishes, silverware, and glasses into the canal—although it appears that a net was stretched across the surface of the water so that nothing would be irretrievably lost.

Towards the middle of the century, Giambattista Tiepolo, the most brilliant Venetian painter of his time, decorated the banquet rooms. In the main hall and on the ceilings of the two adjacent rooms are superb frescoes of mythological subjects, including *Zephyr and Flora*, *The Rape of Persephone*, and *The Life of Cleopatra*. The beauty of the color, the great luminosity, and the force of a style that is at once realistic and magical, place these powerful and vivedly imaginative compositions among the highest achievements of rococo painting.

The large tapestry illustrated on the preceding pages is part of a series of six works showing scenes from the life of Scipion, woven for the Zane family in Brussels in 1650 by Heinry Reydams, Everaert Leyniers, Gerard van der Strecken and Jan van Leefdael. The palace had several owners before being purchased in the twentieth century by Carlos de Beistegui, a wealthy and eccentric Franco-Mexican collector. This refined spiritual heir of the *ancien régime* filled the Palazzo Labia with his magnificent collection of eighteenth-century objets d'art, which were sold at auction after his death. In 1951, Beistegui gave what was perhaps last great reception of the century, attended by the international jet set. For one night, this memorable masked ball revived all the splendor and magic of the era of Goldoni and Casanova. Today, the Palazzo Labia is the headquarters of the RAI, the Italian radio and television company.

67

SCUOLA GRANDE DI SAN GIOVANNI EVANGELISTA

On a small, out-of-the-way *campiello* Gothic grace and Renaissance rigor have been combined in the majestic Scuola di San Giovanni Evangelista, headquarters of one of the six great confraternities of Venice. Created in 1261, this confraternity first used to meet in the Chiesa di Sant'Aponal, before moving in 1301 to the Chiesa di San Giovanni Evangelista, which belonged in part to the Badoer family. This family, one of the most famous in Venice, had already produced five doges for the Republic by the year 1000. The members of the Scuola increased rapidly and, as the confraternity grew in importance, it acquired land next to the church from the Badoers. The current edifice dates from the Gothic period. The beautifully proportioned parvis was built by Pietro Lombardo in 1481 and exalts the relic of the True Cross that Filippo de Masseris, chancellor of the kingdom of Cyprus, gave to the confraternity in 1369. The monumental staircase, built by Mauro Codussi in 1498 in a pure Venetian Renaissance style, is lit by an elegant double window and leads to the chapter house, the largest room in the Scuola. The chapter house took on its present appearance in 1727, when Giorgio Massari transformed it into one of the most elegant baroque interiors in Venice. The beautiful inlaid marble pavement, dating from 1753, is exuberant, measured, and full of light, admirably complementing the paintings by Tintoretto and Giandomenico Tiepolo's luminous ceiling. The same baroque language is used in the superb decorative stuccoes and paintings in the other rooms. But the most representative space of the Scuola is without doubt the Cappella della SS. Croce, redesigned in 1788, which held the precious relic, pride of the confraternity. It was for this chapel that Carpaccio and Mansueti painted their famous large canvases, today conserved in the Accademia.

Chiesa di Santa Maria del Rosario
o Dei Gesuati

In May 1737 Giambattista Tiepolo was commissioned to decorate the ceiling of the Chiesa dei Gesuati, one of the first opportunities he had been given to express his talent to its fullest extent. When the Jesuits were banned from Venice in 1668, the church passed into the possession of the Dominicans, who engaged Tiepolo to paint a cycle commemorating their founder. The ceiling culminates in three frescoes depicting scenes from the life of Saint Dominic. They are particularly admirable for their audacious foreshortening, the spiral movement of the volumes, the immateriality of the transfigured skies, and the elegance of the pinks, grays, and delicate greens which contrast with the well-defined figures in the foreground. The panaches are decorated with sixteen grisailles by the school of Tiepolo illustrating the mysteries of the rosary. In the church, the nave, apsidial chapels, and douple-asped choir are of a luminosity reminiscent of Palladio. This interior space is punctuated by Corinthian engaged columns separated by niches which hold figures of prophets and apostles and bas-reliefs sculpted by Gianmaria Morleiter. The choir, crowned by a cupola, is decorated with frescoes by Tiepolo and the high altar's superb tabernacle is inlaid with lapis lazuli. Finally, there is a beautiful polychrome marble pavement, arranged in intricate geometric motifs.

PALAZZO A SAN POLO

Upon completing *Venezia città nobilissima et singolare* by Francesco Sansovino in 1604, Stringa said of this palace: "It is a superb and unique edifice, but it would have been even more beautiful if it had been built on the Grand Canal." He added that the palace, though reminiscent of the late sixteeenth-century Ca' Bellavitis at San Maurizio, was of recent construction. We know that in 1737 the palace was devastated by fire and that some years later Francesco d'Este, duke of Modena, lived there in exile. Toward the middle of the century, its new owners, proud of their acquisition and their prominent position in the Venetian nobility, had the interior redecorated in a sculptural and pictorial rococo style of sumptuous delicacy, reflecting the latest fashion. The *portego* is animated by an ensemble of stuccoes still characterized by a *horror vacui* typical of the late baroque: a crowded texture of bold, vibrant moldings, plant motifs, and sinuous putti which stand out against backgrounds of solid color. Portraits and cartographic images illustrating an ancestor's maritime expeditions adorn the walls of this vast salon, in which the furniture consists exclusively of pure rococo long benches and pedestal tables. In the elegant early nineteenth-century dining room, the ceiling and wall decoration is directly inspired by Adam, while the sweeping views of gardens and villas recall the contemporary frescoes of Giuseppe Bernardino Bison. The sober eighteenth- and nineteenth-century furniture harmonizes well with the paintings. The private chapel is the secret jewel of the palace; the liturgical furniture, the monochrome paintings offset with gold by Zanchi, and the ceiling frescoes by Francesco Zugno, make it a delightfully rococo place of meditation.

CA' REZZONICO

This colossal baroque edifice, begun in 1667 by Baldassare Longhena for the Priuli-Bon family, rises regally among the buildings along the Grand Canal. The Rezzonicos acquired the palace towards the middle of the eighteenth century, at the very time when the family had the honor of seeing one of its members become pope, in the person of Clement XIII.

The *piano nobile*, reached by the monumental staircase, is dominated by the lavish and theatrical ballroom. The immensity of this room is accentuated by trompe l'œil architectural elements, including balustrades, niches, atlantes and majestic sculptural groups, culminating in an allegorical fresco by Giovan Battista Crosato depicting Apollo's dazzling chariot hurtling into a tumultuous baroque sky. In addition to the sculptures, the sumptuous furnishings lining the walls formed part of the famous set of forty pieces made between 1700 and 1723 by Brustolon for the Venier de San Vio family. Brustolon was an incomparable craftsman specializing in

precious hardwoods, such as ebony and boxwood, and his creations in this palace include impressive statues of Moors, fantastic armchairs supported by slaves and covered in volutes, and monumental console tables carved with chained captives and river gods upon which superb Chinese vases are displayed. Two chandeliers of gilded wood and metal are the only remaining items of earlier furniture. The "Tiepolo room," so called because of the ceiling painting which used to hang at the Palazzo Barbarigo, contains more armchairs by Brustolon, the arms decorated with elegant, slender female figures in boxwood, still upholstered in their original fabric. The other pieces of furniture in this room include a pier-table made of burr with engraved mirrors, an eighteenth-century cabinet with ornamental motifs in gilded silver, and a walnut table with eight legs, while on the the walls, small Venetian-school paintings and a portrait of Alessandro Longhi alternate with large rococo mirrors.

PALAZZO PISANI MORETTA

The economically and politically powerful San Polo branch of the Pisani family commissioned a number of magnificent buildings in and around Venice. These include the country palace at Montagnana by Andrea Palladio, the Palladian villa at Bagnolo, and the ethereal yet robust Rocca Pisana at Lonigo. The Palazzo Pisani in Venice, with its delicate, simple Gothic forms and refined seventeenth- and eighteenth-century interior decoration, survives today thanks to the attentive care of the current owners who have preserved and added to the original furnishings. Towards the middle of the eighteenth century, Chiara Pisani decided to have the different rooms totally refurbished in the new rococo style. The vast and sumptuous *portego*, which today is used as a ballroom, opens onto the Grand Canal via a high Gothic loggia. The walls are decorated with marbled Corinthian pilasters, candelabra with foliated scrolls, and decorative bands of gilded stucco garlands; four large mirrors and rich overdoors complete the decor. The ceiling, with its sophisticated *quadratura*, features a luminous fresco by Jacopo Guarana of a sky filled with graceful figures. Superb eighteenth-century Murano glass chandeliers illuminate the *portego* with their theatrical candlelight.

BIBLIOTECA DI SAN LAZZARO DEGLI ARMENI

In 1717, a community of Roman Catholic Armenian monks settled on the little island of San Lazzaro close to the Lido. In 1789 they set up a printing house, and today continue to publish works in various languages on the long and sometimes tragic history of their people. The community was founded by the monk Manug di Pietro, known as Mekhitar ("The Consoler"), who, fleeing Modon before the advancing Turks, was the first to arrive on the deserted island, which had been the site of a twelfth-century leper colony. The monastery was protected by the Republic and supported by donations from Armenians throughout the world. The buildings are set in a large, peaceful garden where wandering multicolored peacocks serve as reminders of the Orient. The cloister is dominated by an enormous cedar of Lebanon and is a veritable *hortus conclusus*, perfumed by a multitude of roses. This oasis of peace, rich with memories of an extraordinary past, was one of Byron's favorite retreats during his turbulent stay in Venice. The Biblioteca—the monastery library—is a treasure trove reflecting the composite elements that form the community's unique cultural tradition. Eighteenth-century stuccoes and frescoes by Francesco Zugno decorate the ceiling, and the glass-fronted bookcases carved with Ionic pilasters contain several thousand fine old books. An eclectic collection of objects includes a bust of Gregory XVI by Giuseppe Fabris, an eaglet by Antonio Canova, and the mummy of the Egyptian prince Nekmekhet, adorned with a dense network of small pearls. A room furnished with nineteenth-century glass bookcases crowned by small, graceful typana, is dedicated to the memory of *Childe Harold's* author, who shares the space with a beautiful ecclesiastical rostrum and a magnificent eighteenth-century Indian throne inlaid with precious ivory. This throne once belonged to the shah of Persia and is a reminder of an ancient history originating in the Orient.

Palazzo Minotto-Barbarigo

Two successive renovations, in 1744 and 1787, completely transformed the decor of the *piano nobile* of this palace, whose tall Gothic windows look out onto the Grand Canal. A number of major eighteenth-century artists participated in the work, which resulted in a delightfully refined rococo ensemble that exemplified an innovative artistic current that was freer and more imaginative than the rigid schemas of the baroque. In 1745 Giambattista Tiepolo painted a large allegory of *Virtue and Nobility Vanquishing Ignorance* for the ceiling of the salon and the original can be seen today at the Ca' Rezzonico. This large canvas was surrounded by monochrome paintings in lavish stucco frames of the sciences (now in a private collection). Tencalla's sculptural decorations for the overdoors depict allegories of painting, music, and architecture, while the long panoplies of the ceiling exhibit the Ticinese artist's characteristic poetic motifs. The material, however, is less

dramatically prominent, which endows these elements— which all have a distinctly eighteenth-century grace—with new delicacy and harmony. The furniture, lamps, and paintings are also eighteenth century, while superb golden-yellow brocade from the early nineteenth century covers the walls. It is in the bedroom that the rocaille revolution is most clearly apparent. The room still has the traditional tripartite division of space—a large central alcove flanked by two recesses—but the heavy canopies of the previous century, the profusion of putti and the baroque gildings have all been abandoned for the restraint of slender garlands and refined bouquets of flowers, inspired by French rococo decors. The stuccoes on the ceiling resemble light engravings. Fanciful curves and trellis work surround the allegories of love, the shells, and the putti carved in shallow relief. Maria Donà dalle Rose Franchin looks after this exceptionally unified patrimony with great care.

PALAZETTO PISANI

The Palazetto was acquired by the Pisani family in 1751, a period during which they were enjoying the enormous prestige conferred by Alvise Pisani's appointment as doge in 1735. The palace had previously belonged to Giovanni Poleni, physicist, mathematician, astronomer, and a professor at the University of Padua, a personality so famous in Venice that when he died in 1761, the Senate had a medal struck commemorating his scientific achievements. Following his death, in the absence of direct heirs, the palace became the property of the Lazara family, as did the two superb villas at Bagnolo and Lonigo, and is currently owned by an aristocratic family from Padua. The rooms are elegantly furnished and possess beautiful, lavishly decorated wooden ceilings. In the dining room, the blue and gold coffered ceiling is typically baroque and a collection of antique ceramics includes a magnificent Barbarigo-Pisani wedding service. The portraits of eighteenth-century noblewomen in the green salon evoke the illustrious past of the Palazetto's former owners, and the furnishings include two small rococo armchairs and a Venetian rococo commode. On the large oriental carpet, a divan and two armchairs, upholstered in a pink fabric from the Fortuny factory, contrast with the green walls and the late eighteenth-century marquetry divan, above which hangs a large baroque canvas depicting a procurator of the Republic dressed in his bright red gown of office.

PALAZZO GRIMANI

In the eighteenth century, the Palazzo Grimani already possessed the beautiful classical form, inspired by the architecture of Scamozzi, that we still admire today. The property of the Civran family, the palace became the home of the Grimanis, an illustrious Venetian noble family, in 1818. Due to the palace's location on the canal—traditional crew competitions continue to finish under its windows—it appears in works by numerous seventeenth- and eighteenth-century artists, from Coronelli to Canaletto and Carlevarijs. A 1741 engraving by Michele Mariechschi of a regatta on the Grand Canal shows the palace almost exactly as it appears today. Gregorio Lazzarini, Tiepolo's teacher, lived in this palace for many years. The different rooms, magnificently preserved, are rich in eighteenth-century furniture and objects. The dining room is charmingly decorated with

rococo stucco volutes around which flow elegant floral designs while two mirrors the reflect the light cast by bracket lamps made of Murano glass. From the handsome chairs to the two marble-top console tables, all the furniture is Venetian and dates from the eighteenth century. The large library, to which the famous *Grimani Breviary* used to belong, reflects the family's cultural tradition. Comprising some 831 illuminated pages, this fifteenth- and sixteenth-century Flemish breviary is today one of the jewels of the Biblioteca Marciana. The Grimanis had several other residences on the lagoon, including a palace in the style of Sanmicheli at San Luca and the imposing structure on the Rio di Santa Maria Formosa, which had originally been built for Vettore Grimani and his brother Giovanni, patriarch of Aquileia.

PALAZZO BARBARIGO

In 1655 Saint Gregorio Barbarigo was born in this palace built along the Grand Canal, which is composed of two distinct buildings. The nobleman Pietro had the interior refurbished in a rococo style in 1744. As a result of recent meticulous restoration, the mezzanine floor, illuminated by reflections from the Grand Canal, has the peaceful charm of an eighteenth century that was refined rather than sumptuous, evoking the elegance of Mozart's *Divertimenti*. The salon has a typically Venetian *a terrazzo* floor while the walls and ceiling are covered with elegant, slender bas-relief stuccoes in delicate pink, water green, and cream, along with sinuously curving foliated scrolls, tracery, garlands, and stylized cockatoos highlighted or outlined in gold. The series of engravings by Pietro Longhi

of hunting scenes replaced the canvases that Longhi had executed specially for this room, today in the Pinacoteca Querini Stampalia. Four other hunting scenes occupy the corners of the ceiling, while the center is dominated by a painting of *Diana and Endymion*. Above the fireplace in the adjoining room is a rococo mirror, and the Venetian lacquer mantelpiece is decorated with chinoiserie tiles from the Cozzi porcelain factory. The room is lit by two beautiful lights with engraved mirrors and plates with *Blauer Löwe* motifs from the Antonibon factory. The elegant alcove contains four splendid doors whose lower panels, decorated by Jacopo Amigoni, display allegories painted on a black background framed by delicate bouquets.

CHIESA DELLA PIETA O DELLA VISITAZIONE

Founded in the fifteenth century and rebuilt by Giorgio Massari between 1744 and 1760, the Chiesa della Pietà was associated with an adjacent hospital, created in 1346, which assisted needy orphaned girls to receive a musical education paid for by the Republic. The concerts given there were very popular, notably those under the direction of Antonio Vivaldi, who was choirmaster of the chapel from 1703. The church, built on a beautiful oval plan, has a large vault designed for perfect acoustics.

The choir has an elegant marble high altar with a retable by Giambattista Piazetta and his assistant Giuseppe Angeli, and a fresco by Tiepolo depicting the theological virtues decorates the ceiling. On the lateral walls, which are dominated by vast tripartite bays inspired by ancient Roman baths, or *thermae*, are altars framed by coupled pilasters and suspended tribune galleries with fine wrought-iron grills. Until the fall of the Republic, these tribunes, like the one above the entrance to the church, were occupied by the famous "girls' choirs," whose superb singing delighted both Venetians and visiting foreigners such as Charles de Brosses. Three other hospitals in the city also gave similar concerts of sacred music.

PALAZZO MOCENIGO

An imposing edifice located between the Salizzada San Stae and the Grand Canal, the palace was probably built during the sixteenth century, although it did not acquire its current appearance until the eighteenth century. The Mocenigos, one of the oldest and most powerful families of the Serenissima, also owned the two neighboring palaces overlooking the Grand Canal at San Samuele. The San Stae branch of the family kept the residence until 1954, when Alvise Nicolo, the last hereditary owner, bequeathed the palace to the city of Venice. Everything in the palace seems to have been designed to celebrate the glory of the Mocenigos, from the sumptuous furniture and portraits of the sovereigns in whose courts various family members served as ambassadors of Venice, to the busts of the Mocenigo doges and great captains that proudly line the majestic entrance hall. The rooms of the palace, now uninhabited, have been perfectly preserved. In a salon magnificently hung with red, the sumptuous eighteenth-century gilded furniture is reflected in a beautiful *a terrazzo* floor edged with floral motifs. On the ceiling, the fresco by Giacomo Guarana, *The Apotheosis of the Mocenigos*, pays tribute to the illustrious family. The allegorical figures carved on the spectacular baroque frame by Antonio Corradini have been offering laurel crowns and playing silent triumphal music on their trumpets for two centuries, and seem to watch over the solemn portrait of the procurator Giuliano Contarini. A large and equally spectacular mirror at the other end of the room is decorated with two lavishly sculpted mermaids holding the family crest, a reference to the Monicego's maritime accomplishments. The same coat of arms reappears in the panoply above the picture to the right of the mirror, in an unending homage to a grandeur that remained unextinguished by the passage of time.

NINETEENTH-CENTURY ECLECTICISM

The dying embers of the glittering eighteenth century went out with the fall of the Republic, and a mantle of silence fell over Venice. Mortally wounded by no longer being the capital of an independent state, the city closed in on itself. Some of the oldest families deliberately allowed their lines to die out rather than face the disintegration of their entire world. The palaces, empty and silent, fell into disrepair as did the conventual buildings which had been nationalized and stripped of their artistic treasures. Artists and architects like Giannantonio Selva and Guiseppe Borsato carried out Napoleonic building programs around the lagoon. The *Palazzo Reale*, the *Giardini*, the *Archivio di Stato* and the *Accademia* are examples of the Venetian neoclassical genre, which was harsh and simplistic compared with what was being produced throughout the rest of Italy but nevertheless evocative of an unforgettably important past.

The Restoration, the still and tormented years of Hapsburg rule and the birth of Romanticism all combined to relegate Venice to the realms of myth: a myth made up of a longing for past glories and a bloodless aesthetic passion for present decline.

The hagiography of Venice, a watery and fabulous city, transformed into a ghostly Pre-Raphealite Ophelia and an ideal backdrop for obscure Gothic tales and magical Lisztian musical atmospheres, is expressed through a return to a number of traditional Venetian styles. Boito, Meduna and Cadorin refined and blended together the Byzantine, the flamboyant Gothic and the Lombardic Renaissance vocabularies. Many of the canals were filled in, altering the focal points of the city, and it was even proposed that the Grand Canal should be drained so as to enable the railway line to reach the Piazza San Marco.

The international tourists made Venice their favorite destination. Henry James, Browning, Sargent, Paul Bourget, and Wagner followed in the footsteps of Turner and Ruskin. This led to the building of the grand hotels, and the Lido, progenitor of the second wave of Romantic architecture, was created out of nothing. Its fantastic revival of flamboyant Gothic and Moorish styles, set quite apart from the rest of the historic city, created a completely new cipher which in turn led to the burgeoning of art nouveau, the creations of Torres and Sullam and the sumptuous orientalism of the *Hotel Excelsior*.

The interiors reflect the eclecticism of the nineteenth century: the algid and sophisticated elegance of the formal neoclassical spaces gave way to Romantic *pastiches*. A bourgeois yet visionary solution of a Venice historicized through its various epochs, frequently brilliantly and dramatically flung together, embodied the sophisticated and decadent world evoked in the works of Proust and Fortuny.

Palazzo Belloni Battagia

The Palazzo Belloni Battagia, with its monumental baroque façade, is a perfect example of what during that period was called the "true style," otherwise known as neoclassicism. In 1804, the residence was radically modernized by the new owner Antonio Capovilla, who had purchased it from the Battagia family. An extremely wealthy merchant, Capovilla spent one hundred thousand ducats, an incredible sum at the time, to transform the palace. In fact, new imperatives of comfort required that the enormous traditional *portego* be shortened and the size of the rooms reduced with false ceilings, a process which also allowed the "rational" ideas, which were causing such a stir in the world of architecture, to be incorporated.

The walls and ceilings were painted with frescoes by the most fashionable decorators working in Venice and the surrounding regions at the turn of the century. Giambattista Canal, a fresco painter known as "the last *fà presto*" (an allusion to the speed of painters in the preceding century), and the ornamentist David Rossi created an entrance hall in which trompe l'œil triumphs. Space is extended illusionistically in a pictorial universe that includes a theatrical portico composed of a double row of columns between which are scenes inspired by Homer. The cool colors and the symmetrical arrangement of the figures, which combine echoes of Tiepolo with novel elements taken from Canova, show that international neoclassicism had now triumphed in Venice. One finds this same decorative language, this time with Anglo-French connotations, in a room overlooking the Grand Canal. False bas-reliefs painted in monochrome, recalling Mantegna's *Trionfi*, adjoin ceiling stuccoes inspired by the creations of the English ceramicist Josiah Wedgwood. The entire composition, in shades of white and pale blue, is accentuated by gilded circles set in a geometric network of fine moldings which conclude with elegant, abstract, Empire-style stucco fans.

Ala Napoleonica

Napoleonic rule naturally demanded a regal residence, a dazzling symbol befitting the power of the new ruler. Work started on the Procuratie Nuove, where apartments had been created for the imperial family in 1807, and continued on the short side of the Palazzo San Marco with the demolition of the Chiesa di San Geminiano, built by Sansovino. In its place, a new section, known as the Ala Napoleonica (the Napoleon wing), was built, similar in style to the Procuratie Nuove. In 1813 a magnificent staircase was added in keeping with the opulence of the imperial regime, along with a vast ballroom inspired by the Empire style imported from France and disseminated by the engravings of Percier and Fontaine. Giuseppe Borsato, the great proponent of Venetian neoclassicism, was responsible for all the decoration and the original furniture. In the long narrow ballroom, the musicians' gallery is composed of hemicycles with half-domes and white and gold Corinthian columns, while the rest of the room is decorated with fluted pilasters, projecting cornices, sophisticated Roman-style motifs within rigorous geometric frames, garlands, Greek key patterns, false bas-reliefs of putti in grisaille, as well as the lyre and laurel wreath, attributes of Apollo, which recall the musical and symbolic functions of the ballroom. The wide band decorating the curvature of the ceiling is painted with elegant trompe l'œil coffers in shades of gold and pearl gray.

Palazzo Loredan

Originally a Gothic building belonging to the Mocenigo family, the palazzo has a long, serene Renaissance façade, which used to be decorated with frescoes depicting episodes from Roman history by Salviati and an unknown Florentine master. It became part of the Loredan patrimony in 1536. The Loredan family entrusted the reconstruction to Antonio Abbondi, known as Scarpignano, but the work was completed by Giovanni Grapiglia, a pupil of Scamozi, between 1700 and 1720. When the last Loredan of Santa Stefano, Francesco Loredan, became doge in 1752, Domenico Scarlatti commemorated the event in music set to a text by Goldoni, but his tenure is remembered for its lavishness rather than for its achievements. Around 1805, the palace was bought by the wealty entrepreneur Giacomo Berti, who in turn sold it to the Napoleonic administration. During the years of Hapsburg rule, the palace became the headquarters of the city's Imperial Command and later that of the Venetian Institute of Arts and Letters, founded by the Austrian emperor Francis I. Inside, a gigantic entrance hall leads to the prestigious library which contains an precious collection of periodicals. The *alla sansovina* ceiling and sophisticated eighteenth-century Murano chandelier recall the former splendor of these silent rooms. The "sala nuova," built in 1589, is dominated by a portal with a magnificent marble pediment, probably by Grapiglia, who also created the original decoration of this room, where the Institute holds its academic meetings. The ceiling used to feature an ornate baroque decorative program, since lost, by the Brescian artist Filippo Zaniberti. Inspired by the mannered poems of Giambattista Marino and the myth of Adonis, it stupified Zaniberti's contemporaries with its virtuosity. The black and gold furniture, which, like the wall decoration, dates from the nineteenth century, conceals the graceful design of the *a terrazzo* pavement. The room is lit by a large Murano glass chandelier. On the end wall, between two windows, hangs an austere, monumental painting by Tintoretto.

Teatro La Fenice

The neoclassical theater by Antonio Selva was inaugurated on 16 May 1792 with Giovanni Paisiello's opera *Giochi d'Agrigento*. The interior was designed by Costantino Cedini, Francesco Fontanesi and Pietro Gonzaga. The ceiling painting of the *Triumph of Apollo* by Giambattista Canal and Giuseppe Borsato in the auditorium was not completed until 1808, following the restoration carried out during the previous year on the occasion of Napoleon's arrival in Venice. Borsato retouched the ceiling in 1828 but, nearly ten years later, a fire devastated the theater and the directors were forced to rebuild, a task they entrusted to the engineers Tommaso and Giambattista Meduna and the ornamentist Tranquillo Orsi. Giambattista Meduna won the design competition launched in 1854 and he created the current neo-rococo decoration. Conceived in a fanciful eighteenth-century style, the auditorium is covered from one end to the other with luxurious gold arabesques, culminating with the royal box, built in 1866. Medallions and putti by Leonardo Gavagnin, who also produced the groups of figures on the ceiling, and the delicate flowers by Giuseppe Voltan stand out against the gold of the boxes. The sumptuous decoration of this theater was an attempt to recover the lost splendor of the Serenissima, the magnificence of a mythic golden age revived here in a dazzling atmosphere, more French than Venetian, which anticipates the pompous châteaux that Ludwig II would build in Bavaria at the end of the century. The unforgettable scene in Luchino Visconti's film *Senso*, in which the patriots throw hundreds of leaflets and rosettes onto the floor to the cry of "Vive Verdi," may well refer to the thirteen years that the composer spent working at La Fenice, the period during which he produced *Ernani*, in 1844, followed by *La Traviata* and *Rigoletto*. Beginning in 1930 the theater was used for the International Festival of Contemporary Music, and works by Igor Stravinsky and Benjamin Britten were given their first performances here, as were more recent compositions by Nono, Berio and Sylvano Bussotti.

CAFFE FLORIAN

The craze for coffee—a drink inherited from the Ottoman Empire—spread across Europe with stunning rapidity. Johann Sebastian Bach's wild, ironic *Coffee Cantata*, in which a delighted Liesgen consents to marry when her future husband promises her his precious "brown potion," testifies to this immoderate passion. In 1683, the same year that Eugene of Savoy's victory under the walls of Vienna effectively ended the Ottoman's westward expansion, the first Venetian "coffee shop" was opened under the arcades of the Procuratie. Others soon appeared all over the city and, a century later, Venice had so many that there were twenty-four cafés around the Piazzo San Marco alone. "Every arcade is the entrance to a café which is never empty," noted President de Brosses in his travel notebook. In 1720, one such establishment, the Alla Venezia Trionfante ("To Venice Triumphant"), opened its doors under the arcades of the Procuratie Nuove, and its owner was Floriano Francesconi. This café was soon known as the Florian and quickly became a literary and social meeting place. Regulars included

the Gozzi brothers and Carlo Goldoni, who, in 1736, wrote a famous interlude entitled *Le bottega del caffè*. In 1858, Lodovico Cadorin redecorated the succession of rooms in the fashionable style of the time with gilded dark mahogany, small garnet-red velvet divans and light marble tables. Cadorin, who had already designed the Quadri, a neighboring café, with an eclectic and elegant verve, created a unique atmosphere based on an original layout and careful attention to the smallest details. These rooms, whose design reflected the fashions and revival styles of the day, did not neglect the demand for comfort that was a growing preoccupation of bourgeois society. Scenes and figures painted on glass by Pascutti,Casa, Carlini, Battistuzzi, set in foliated scrolls in grisaille and large mirrors with fine Arabic motifs help to create an inimitable ambience in this café, which is at once "a stock market, a theater foyer, a reading room, a club and a confessional," as another regular, Honoré de Balzac, once wrote.

Casa Frollo alla Giudecca

The large kitchen at the Casa Frollo—an exclusive guesthouse located outside the city on the island of Giudecca with a passionate and protective local clientele—provides a glimpse of the traditional way of life which, not so long ago, the people of the lagoon used to lead. This typical Venetian kitchen is dominated by the vast hood over the stoves, grills and small frying pans, an indispensable element in local cooking. The brilliant copper pans and implements bring the room to life: coffee pots, dripping pans, casseroles, ladles, caldrons and, of course, classic water jugs made of spun copper—an essential item in the classic Venetian kitchen—hang in tight rows above the hearth. In the center of the room, which is paved *a terrazzo*, is a large table with a marble top surrounded by Thonet chairs.

Palazzo Dandolo

In 1840, a mysterious adventurer, Giuseppe Dal Niel, otherwise known as "Danieli," bought this Gothic residence from the Mocenigo family. He had been renting the palace since 1822 and had already transformed it into what would become, over the course of the century, the Venetian hotel par excellence. Magnificently situated on the Riva degli Schiavoni, a stone's throw from the Piazza San Marco, this palace often appears in eighteenth- and nineteenth-century *vedute*, from the precise views of Canaletto to the romantic, snow-covered landscapes of Giuseppe Borsato. The Danieli, as it is known, immediately became popular with the growing number of wealthy, cosmopolitan tourists in search of an Italy more imaginary than real, as portrayed in literature, the Gothic dreams of Ruskin, the romances of Wagner and the hackneyed, historicist paintings of the time. In 1840 Tranquillo Orsi was commissioned to decorate the hotel. Three years earlier, Orsi had collaborated on the refurbishment of La Fenice but he died before the work on the hotel was finished. The monumental neo-medieval entrance hall, a soaring vertical space, is typical, in its decorative excess, of the second half of the nineteenth century. The enormous golden staircase, Byzantine lamps, galleries with minutely adorned Moorish arches, balustrades with thin, oriental colonnettes are all elements of the academic repertory of a decadent Venice, sinking in its own nostalgia, erudition, and weariness. Nearly all the late nineteenth-century sovereigns of Europe stayed at the Danieli, and other illustrious guests included Dickens, Balzac, D'Annunzio, and Proust. As for George Sand, an episode of her notorious and stormy affair with Alfred de Musset took place at the Danieli.

PALAZZO PESARO DEGLI ORFEI

This superb Gothic palace, the property of the noble
Pesaro family, was known as the "degli Orfei" after 1786,
when it became the headquarters of the Apollinea
Philharmonic Society. This society, which was later
transferred to La Fenice, organized concerts, operas and large
balls. The Spanish painter Mariano Fortuny y Madrazo, a
Wagnerian set designer and inventor of the famous stage
"cupola," continued this musical tradition when he bought
the palace at the end of the last century and made it his main
residence. The opulent, eclectic interior is still imprinted with
the sumptuous and strange atmosphere created by the artist.
Theatrical hangings create spaces which break up the Gothic
rhythm of the building; on the walls, tapestries with
Renaissance, Arabic, Chinese and Persian motifs create
a nineteenth-century orientalist world which has been grafted
onto an omnipresent theme, that of the unique

history of Venice. The Tiepoloesque Cleopatra, inspired
by the frescoes in the Palazzo Labia, is by Fortuny
himself, and, like the numerous other copies in the palace,
is a delightful decorative element. Reproductions of classical
statues are silhouetted against the loggia, and the ensemble
is lit by a lamp created by this multi-talented artist.
A sofa with colorful cushions stands in front of a diaphaneous
red wall hanging decorated with Renaissance motifs; the
cushions are covered with Fortuny fabrics printed with a
wooden stamp using a technique inspired by photography.
Among the other paintings by Mario Fortuny
is a Goya-inspired portrait of Mrs. Fortuny dressed
as a *maja*. This salon, so evocative of decadentism,
is an ideal setting for the narrations of D'Annunzio,
the steamy seductions of the *Tales of Hoffman* or Proust's
Albertine imagining a "Venice saturated with the Orient."

TWENTIETH-CENTURY DEBATE

The progress of modern Venetian architecture has been troubled and contradictory. Until the end of the 1950s, the city was the scene of artistic and musical innovation (the famous saga of the Biennale and its pavilions; the great musical premières, of Stravinsky's *Rake's Progress* for example; Peggy Guggenheim's avant-garde artistic coteries), but Venice staunchly refused to admit styles and trends alien to her historic traditions. Significantly, the works of Wright and Le Corbusier, two of the greatest modern architects, were deemed unacceptable.

The Lido, which at the beginning of the twentieth century had moved on from the rarefied and twilight atmospheres of Thomas Mann to the jazz age, welcoming Diaghilev and Nijinsky, Lifar and Rubinstein, Jean Renoir and Coco Chanel, seems to have been the major forum for architectural debate. But even here, innovations were scarcely given room: during the twenty years of Fascist rule, markedly rationalist buildings like the garage on Piazzale Roma and the Santa Lucia railway station were confined to the outer edges of the city. There was an attempt at compromise between the modern architectural vocabulary and the millenary historical heritage, the only possible way forward being the contemporary treatment of traditional elements, Ignazio Gardella's house on the Zattere being a prime example.

Interiors were the only places where modern trends were allowed to flourish and the architect Carlo Scarpa was the most talented designer of them all. Scarpa was an unusual blend of artist and craftsman and he used classical materials like Istrian stone, glass, and metal which he combined with rugged concrete, inventing clever architectural solutions to create abstract, elegant spaces.

Echoes of the city's architectural vocabulary were combined with exotic oriental influences, Japanese Zen in particular, upon which Venice continued to draw as a source of inspiration. Venice's present-day interior architecture is still dominated by Scarpa's influence, although its solutions are infinite and eclectic. Contemporary culture seems to have lost all points of reference, and even the vocabulary of the interior appears to move freely between philological or ironic references to Venice's unforgettable past and minimalist conceptual environments, or indeed the more *recherché* forms of international design, although it never quite loses the unmistakable and magical imprint of the intrinsic essence of Venice.

The Austrian Pavilion at the Venice Biennale

HARRY'S BAR

The adventure of this legendary restaurant began on 13 May 1931, when Giuseppe Cipriani and his associate Harry Pickering, a young American relying on his own incomparable experience in the art of bartending, rented a building which, until that time, had been used as a rope storehouse. They enlisted the aid of Baron Gianni Rubin de Cervin, who painted marine subjects on the walls and selected the art deco furniture, including vast armchairs—later replaced by smaller ones which were less cumbersome and more practical—tables with three legs for greater stability and a long counter near the entrance to receive customers. Cipriani introduced many innovations, from the use of light

to enhance the interior to the elegant and restrained decor which broke with the stifling atmosphere of the classic luxury restaurants of the previous century. The dishes and silverware, simple in design, were chosen for functional reasons, making it easier to provide service that was meticulous and attentive but relaxed. It is impossible to name all the political and artistic personalities and members of international society who have frequented Harry's Bar, but they included Toscanini, Somerset Maugham, Guglielmo Marconi and, of course, Ernest Hemingway, who was the undisputed king of the establishment in the period immediately following the Second World War.

HOTEL EXCELSIOR

The imposing Grand Hotel Excelsior, the first hotel of its size on the Venetian coast, is located on the Lido, a long, thin strip of sand which separates the lagoon from the open sea. In the nineteenth century it was secluded and romantic, imbued with an atmosphere that attracted restless spirits such as Lord Byron and Shelley. At the dawn of the following century it became the favorite winter retreat for a new generation of refined and elegant international tourists which Thomas Mann evoked nostalgically in *Death in Venice*. The Lido became an exclusive resort, enjoying the prestige of Deauville, Biarritz and Cabourg—Proust's Balbec—or the French Riviera, which was frequented in the 1920s by the cosmopolitan jazz-age society portrayed in the works of F. Scott Fitzgerald. The Hotel Excelsior was designed by Giovanni Sardi half a century after the first Lido bath house opened. The architecture combines Veneto-Byzantine echoes with an Arabian-Moorish style and is closely related to that of the great hotels of the period such as the Grand Hotel de Cairo. The large, bright, luxurious dining room was designed to satisfy a sophisticated and affluent clientele. The stucco coffers on the ceiling, the arch over the entrance, the large chandeliers, and the marble columns all accentuate the hotel's formality. The Louis XIV-style furniture was typical of the grand hotels of the period, although the Empire-style would become more popular later in the century.

Negozio Olivetti

One of the most successful and refined examples of modern architecture in Venice, the Negozio Olivetti occupies a long, narrow space under the sixteenth-century Renaissance arcades of the Procuratie Vecchie, which served as the official the residence of the Procurators of San Marco until 1797.

In 1957, the industrialist Adriano Olivetti, always open to innovation, commissioned Carlo Scarpa to redesign his business premises. Scarpa's balanced and lively use of space is characterized by a harmonious interplay of different materials. The perfectly smooth plaster outlined by wood and the geometric rigor of the stone staircase and the slab fountain—water is a recurring element in Scarpa's work— have been combined with the roughness of concrete and the refined Murano glass tesserae of the pavement, arranged in a four-color mosaic based on a design by Paul Klee that simulates the optical effects produced by the yearly Venetian natural phenomenon of the spring tide and its attendant floods.

Casa Mainella

Carlo Scarpa's involvement with the interior of this nineteenth-century building began in 1964 and continued for nearly ten years. The architect has successfully resolved the difficult problem of creating a residence that can also serve as an exhibition space. The different collections of the investment partners—Persian ceramics, classical statues, Renaissance furniture and contemporary works— are enhanced by an architectural design as imaginative as it is rigorous, in which each sequence functions as an autonomous element, controlled down to the smallest detail. The beautiful geometrical curve of the staircase, which spirals around a monumental central pillar, is sculpturally defined by the light, which models the forms. The white marble of the steps, echoed by the thin stone slabs of the podium, are juxtaposed with the ivory marbling of the walls. This design, typical of Carlo Scarpa's architectural style, displays a complete freedom of expression, and through the use of centuries-old materials and techniques, simultaneously combines modernity with Venetian artistic traditions.

Fondazione Querini Stampalia

Count Giovanni, last descendant of the Querini Stampalia family, bequeathed his palace (left and right) to the city of Venice in 1868. Today the building houses a major library and a museum located in rooms that during mid-nineteenth century were the apartments of the Venetian patriarch. Between 1961 and 1963 the ground floor of this Renaissance palace was totally transformed by Carlo Scarpa, who designed an exhibition room and an entrance hall. In the latter, two large, identical grills which fill the ground-floor arches allow natural light and air to penetrate freely. The beautiful surface of the floor is made up of marbles in three different colors and stops at the edge of the contrasting "dyke," made of stone and cement. Behind this low wall, a deep channel, filled by the waters of the spring tides, lightens and amplifies the geometry of the different spaces, embroidering the severe fabric of the marbles and the simple weave of the exposed bricks like a fine gold ribbon. A path running parallel to the water crosses the different rooms before being broken up in the central area into a sort of architectural origami—an interplay of cubes set one inside the other—forming a staircase leading to the canal and establishing a link with the Zen-like course of the water, bare and labyrinthine, in the garden situated to the rear of the palace.

Casa a San Sebastiano
(Following page)

It was in this small, elegant sixteenth-century palace that Ignatius of Loyola and Saint Francis Xavier celebrated their first masses. The two events probably took place in the salon, which was used as a chapel during the sixteenth century and where the ceiling is decorated with a fresco, now severely altered, representing an allegory of the Catholic faith. More recently, the palace was inhabited by the painter Guido Cadorin. Upon his death, the building underwent drastic modification and the layout was radically changed. Meticulous restoration was the keynote of interior designer Matteo Corvino's approach, in accordance with his client's wish to restore the refined eighteenth-century atmosphere. The fluid, sensual Venetian light enters the tranquil succession of salons at regular intervals, enhancing their charm. The eye is drawn to the niche at the end of the enfilade where, enigmatic and distant, stands a neoclassical kore in bronze.

Palazzo Albrizzi

This particularly refined home has been created in the attic of the Palazzo Albrizzi, one of the most prestigious palaces in Venice. The two main floors and the mezzanine—decorated between the seventeenth and nineteenth centuries—are of an unparalleled sumptuousness. The massive beams are a key element in this enormous attic, harmonizing with an architectural design whose modernity is highlighted by the abundant light penetrating through the numerous openings. In the salon, the geometric pattern of the floor, with its distant echo of classical Venetian decor, pays homage to the style of Carlo Scarpa, adapted to the particular features of this beautiful space. A strict, functional structure of metal and glass houses the prestigious library, a reminder of the Albrizzi family's role in the history of Venetian publishing in the eighteenth century. This articulate and harmonious interior is discreetly enlivened by seventeenth-century portraits and antique furniture. In the dining area, the light plays over the brilliant carmine walls in geometric shapes reminiscent of the paintings of Mark Rothko. Anton Webern felt that "the first duty of the analyst consists in showing the functions of the different parts," and he added, "themes are secondary." That is the lesson, inscribed in space with its planes and its lines, taught by the old staircase leading to the *altana* or roof-terrace.

PALAZZO SERNAGIOTTO

Henry James, who on several occasions stayed for extended periods at the Palazzo Barbaro as a guest of his friend Curtis, was an admirer of this palace, which he felt had a grandeur which was not oppressive. At the end of the nineteenth century, Venice took on a cosmopolitan dimension, becoming the ideal rendezvous for refined society, a city where intellectuals and aristocrats rubbed shoulders and where one could meet the numerous English and American visitors, seduced by the age-old culture of the Serenissima. It was in this spirit, but in a resolutely contemporary style, that the renovation of this palace overlooking the Grand Canal was undertaken. The precious tapestry on the walls contrasts with the simplicity of the natural fiber flooring. Numerous references to the Orient, so closely associated with the history of Venice, have been combined with the luxurious elegance of the Empire furniture, while a large gilded mirror in Murano glass adds a strictly traditional note.

CASA PINTO A SAN VIO

The austere brickwork on the walls of this small nineteenth-century oratory, now the home of an interior designer, is enriched with columns, tripartite niches, precious frames and neo-Byzantine oculi in polychrome marble. The theatrical power of these elements, all part of the original decor, have enabled the unique atmosphere of the building to be preserved, but in a totally contemporary style. The volume of the beautiful old nave has been exploited by the introduction of a light, bare metal mezzanine which, while respecting the original architecture, creates a new living area, where grills, graceful openings and the rigorous geometrical design of the metal beams offer a new interpretation of space. Furniture and objects have been judiciously selected in the prevailing eclectic spirit, and the sophisticated fabrics, the bust of a young man, and the small Thonet table are all fin-de-siècle evocations which contrast intelligently with the elegant, sculptural staircase.

VISITOR'S GUIDE

BYZANTINE TO FLAMBOYANT GOTHIC

CATTEDRALE DI SANTA MARIA ASSUNTA A TORCELLO

ACTV Stop: Torcello
Opening Times:
10 A.M.–12:30 P.M./2–6:30 P.M., closed Sunday. Admission charge.

See of the Bishop of Altino from the seventh century until the fall of the Republic, the cathedral was rebuilt and restored in 864 and again in 1008. The Veneto-Byzantine church dates from the eleventh century and the basilical plan is evidence of continuing strong cultural links with Rome. The façade with its pilaster strips was erected in the eleventh century and is preceded by a portico, lengthened in the fourteenth century. There are unusually fine Veneto-Byzantine and Ravenna mosaics in the central apse. The marble geometric mosaic work pavements and ambulatory are superb, while the Bishop's throne, placed high in the presbytery apse at the top of some handsome steps, is very imposing.

BASILICA DEI SANTI MARIA E DONATO A MURANO

Address: Murano, Fondamenta Giustiniani
ACTV Stop: Murano, Museo Vetrario
Opening Times: 8 A.M.–12 P.M./4–7 P.M.

As at Torcello, the church was built around the seventh century, at the time of the first settlements on the islands of

the lagoon, and enlarged and altered to a basilical plan sometime after the year 1000. The main façade, in terse Ravenna style, has Roman lapidiary stones beneath the side pillars. Camillo Boito's restoration (1858–1873) took the external walls back to the brick and there are some large beveled niches. The hexagonal apse bears carved panels and pulvinated capitals together with lapidary fragments from the earlier construction. Paintings by Lazzaro Bastiani and Marco Vecellio and a thirteenth-century painting thought to be by Paolo Veneziano are among the works possessed by the church.

CLOISTER OF SANT'APOLLONIA

Address: Castello 4312, Ponte della Canonica
ACTV Stop: San Zaccaria
Opening Times: 10:30 A.M.–12:30 P.M., closed Sunday

A unique thirteenth-century cloister, this Romanesque structure is the only one of its kind on the Venetian mainland, and once formed the entrance to the Benedictine Convent, thought to have been founded during the twelfth, thirteenth, or possibly early fourteenth century. The coenoby was placed under the jurisdiction of the Primicerio di San Marco in 1473, and housed the Seminario Ducale between 1579 and 1591. The façade on the Rio was altered by Lorenzo Santi in 1828, and the building used by the Imperial Criminal Tribunal. The collection of Roman, Byzantine and early Venetian lapidary fragments which constitutes the Lapidario Marciano is displayed on the cloister walls. The building is now the home of the Museo Diocesano d'Arte Sacra (Museum of Diocesan Art).

CRYPT OF THE BASILICA DI SAN MARCO

Address: Piazza San Marco
ACTV Stop: San Marco or
San Zaccaria
No admission

The steps going down by the side of the presbytery of the Basilica di San Marco lead to the crypt, which is on a line with the basilica itself and with the two side chapels. In 1094 Saint Mark's body was interred there, while Ordelaf Falier Dodoni was doge. The Confraternita dei Mascoli met behind the high altar from 1222 until the end of the sixteenth century, and it is here that the great stone slab containing the remains of the Evangelist, thought for centuries to have been lost and only discovered during the restorations of 1811, are to be found.

PALAZZO DUCALE

Address: Piazzetta San Marco
ACTV Stop: San Marco or San Zaccaria
Opening Times: 9 A.M.–6 P.M.
Admission charge

There is nothing left of the original

Byzantine building, founded in the ninth century by the Partecipazio, and the present structure was erected in the late thirteenth century. The wing of the Palazzo on the Molo was restored between 1340 and 1365. Its façade is divided horizontally into three fascias. The use of space was revolutionary: at the top is a solid polychrome patterned wall, in the middle the harmonious flowing arches of the loggia, decorated with quatrefoil roundels, and below an arcaded portico supported by heavy engaged columns. The stonemason Filippo Calendario is said to have conceived the design, using a prototype fairly common in Gothic Venice. Certainly the central window, which is a blend of singularly autochthonous elements and Arab-Muslim geometric tracery, quickly became part of the Venetian architectural vocabulary. The great central window in the façade overlooking the Rio, crowned with pinnacles and carvings by the Dalle Masegne, was installed at the beginning of the fifteenth century. The façade overlooking the Piazzetta was completed in 1424 and the late Gothic Porta della Carta added as a finishing touch in 1442. This was the last significant addition to the building's exterior and from then on only the internal spaces and imposing courtyard were subject to any major change.

CHIESA DI SANTO STEFANO

Address: San Marco, Campo Santo Stefano
ACTV Stop: Sant'Angelo, Accademia, or San Samuele
Opening Times: 8 A.M.–12 P.M./4–7 P.M., closed Monday morning

The Augustinian monastic church was completely rebuilt around the middle of the fourteenth century, replacing an earlier thirteenth-century building. Bartolomeo Bon's flamboyant Gothic portal provided the finishing touch at the beginning of the fifteenth century. The interior is fourteenth-century Gothic, the altars bear Lombardic carvings by Alessandro Vittoria, Gerolamo Campagna and Giulio del Moro and there are paintings by Jacopo Marieschi, Leonardo Corona and Nicolo Bambini. Leonardo Scalamanzio's and Marco Cozzi's splendid, grandiose choir stalls have Gothic-style wooden

carvings and inlays; built in 1488, they were originally situated in the middle of the central nave. In the sacristy there are paintings by Palma Vecchio, Paris Bordone, Sante Peranda and three vigorous canvases by Tintoretto: *The Last Supper*, the *Washing of Feet* and *The Agony in the Garden*, all late works. The musician Giovanni Gabrieli is buried in the church and Giovanni Falier's funerary stele, carved in 1808 by Canova, is also located there.

CHIESA DI SANTA MARIA GLORIOSA DEI FRARI

Address: San Polo, Campo dei Frari
ACTV Stop: San Toma
Opening Times: Monday–Saturday 9 A.M.–12 P.M./2:30–6 P.M., admission charge; Sunday 3–5:30 P.M., entry free

In 1234 the minor Franciscan monks received a plot of land in the area known as San Toma as a gift from Giovanni Badoer, and it was here that the first stone of the church was laid on 3 April 1250. The original structure is known to have still been standing in 1415, but it was demolished shortly

after that to make room for the present building, which was consecrated on 27 May 1492. The powerful slant of the walls seems determined to dominate the tripartite façade, crowned by a series of small niches and distinguished by four pilaster strips which mark out the three naves, each of which has a large circular window. The ogival entrance doorway has a sculpture of the Resurrected Christ attributed to Alessandro Vittoria. The interior is cruciform and, in addition to the three naves, there is a transept and a central apse, off which there are three side polygonal apsidial chapels. The church contains a remarkable collection of fine works of art, including Titian's *Pesaro Altarpiece* (completed in 1526), Donatello's wooden statue of *Saint John the Baptist*, Giovanni Bellini's triptych of the *Madonna and Child with Four Saints* in the Sacristy, and Titian's marvelously luminous *Assumption*, commissioned in 1516. Among the many funerary monuments are Titian's and Canova's mausoleums as well as the tomb of Claudio Monteverdi.

RENAISSANCE AND MANNERISM

PALAZZO CORNER SPINELLI

Address: San Marco 3877, Campiello del Teatro
ACTV Stop: Sant'Angelo
Private, no admission

The palace, built by Mauro Codussi circa 1490, features a bifoil crowned by a blind *oculus* and set into a ribbed round arch, introducing a late Gothic note into the otherwise Renaissance vocabulary. The heavily rusticated high plinth has a double row of openings in Tuscan

Humanist style. The interior, remodeled by Michele Sanmicheli in 1542, saw the beginnings of the new, aesthetic, anti-naturalistic style of painting known as mannerism. The panelled perspective ceiling by Vasari with heavily foreshortened figures (now dispersed and in several different collections) was much copied by the new wave of Venetian artists, from Tintoretto to Veronese. The palace belonged to the famous dancer Maria Taglioni during the nineteenth century, and is now owned by the silk manufacturer Lorenzo Rubelli.

PALAZZO CONTARINI DELLE FIGURE

Address: San Marco 3327, Calle Mocenigo
ACTV Stop: Sant'Angelo
Private, no admission

This palace was built betwen 1504 and 1546 on the site of a previous Gothic structure.
The appellation "delle figure" derives from the two monsters crouching beneath the balcony of the *piano nobile*.
The design has been attributed to Scarpignano, but the syntax of the architecture, the tortuous naturalistic lines with their refined panoplies, the proto-mannerist sculptures and the fine classical tympanum which serves as a cornice over the central multifoil are redolent of rather more sophisticated and modern cultural influences, such as the work of the central Italians or even Palladio.
Recorded by Ruskin, the palace contained an abundant collection of works of art until 1713, amongst which was Veronese's *Rape of Europa*.

CHIESA DI SANTA MARIA MATER DOMINI

Address: Santa Croce, Campo Santa Maria Mater Domini
ACTV Stop: San Stae
Opening Times: 10 A.M.–12 P.M./3–5 P.M.

The church, one of the first true Renaissance buildings in the city, was built between 1502 and 1540, its elegant rugged outline reminiscent of Codussi. The design is attributed to Giovanni Buora or indeed to Sansovino, who is said to have completed the building. The interior is greater evidence of his proto-Renaissance imprint, being a compromise between the use of traditional local features such as the Byzantine cupola, and elements imported from central Italy. The church's Renaissance origins are further emphasized by the works of art it contains: sculptures by Lorenzo Bregno, Francesco Bissolo's *Transfiguration* and the translucent, delicate landscapes of Vincenzo Catena's masterpiece, the *Martyrdom of Saint Christina*.

SCUOLA GRANDE DI SAN ROCCO

Address: San Polo 3054, Campo San Rocco
ACTV Stop: San Toma
Opening Times: Weekdays 28 March to 2nd November 9 A.M.–5:30 P.M.
Weekdays 3 November to 27 March 10 A.M.–1 P.M.
Saturday and Sunday 10 A.M.–4 P.M.

The building is the work of several architects—there were three different chief architects in charge of the works at various times. It was erected between 1515 and 1524 by Bartolomeo Bon who was responsible for the overall design and for the ground floor with its precious marbles, its overall

appearance softened by the Codussian bifoils. Sante Lombardo was responsible for the façade on the Rio, and Scarpignano, who directed operations from 1527 to 1549, completed the façade on the *campo*. Guglielmo de'Grigi completed the building in 1560, and the interior boasts Tintoretto's world famous cycle of paintings, begun in 1564 and completed in 1588.

LIBRERIA DI SAN MARCO

Address: Piazzetta San Marco
ACTV Stop: San Marco or San Zaccaria
Visits by appointment only;
reading rooms open 9 A.M.–1 P.M., closed Sunday

The manuscript collection belonging to the Greek Cardinal Bessarione formed the basis for the library. The building was erected by Sansovino between 1537 and 1545, and he continued to work on it until 1554. Vincenzo Scamozzi completed the construction between 1583 and 1588. The façade, which features a double row of engaged columns and elegant mannerist decoration, takes the form of a sweeping longitudinal loggia. A Doric portico is surmounted by an Ionic loggia, surmounted in turn by an elaborate frieze decorated with festoons and putti, above which there is an attic with balustrade and acroteria, and the ensemble is finally crowned by obelisks and mythological sculptures. The interior boasts the monumental *Sala Dorata* with paintings by Andrea Schiavone, Tintoretto, and Veronese among others.

PALAZZO GIUSTINIAN-RECANATI

Address: Dorsoduro 1402
ACTV Stop: Zattere
Private, no admission

The simple, basic late-sixteenth century structure with its rugged main elevation is softened by a central multifoil with rounded cusps. The palace was enlarged at the beginning of the nineteenth century and the *piano nobile* remains unchanged from its austere sixteenth-century design, with superb wooden ceilings and a large

portego, which is entered through a monumental baroque marble doorway. The building contains some very fine works of art, notably Canaletto's *Fonteghetto della Farina* and a small elegant Tiepolo, as well as a considerable collection of books and a prestigious family archive which bears witness to the secular history of the family's close links with the Serenissima.

BASILICA DEL REDENTORE

Address: Giudecca, Fondamenta San Giacomo
ACTV Stop: Redentore
Opening Times: 7 A.M.–12 P.M./4–5 P.M.

Palladio's sanctuary, built between 1577 and 1592, its façade composed of a fine sequence of intersecting floors, rises majestically from the line of low buildings bordering the Giudecca canal. It is an austere structure, with its geometric counterpoint of rectangluar and triangular forms rising from a heavily rusticated podium. Inside, among the paintings decorating the altars, there are works by Pietro Vecchia, Alvise Vivarini, Lazzaro Bastiani, Francesco Bassano the Younger, and *The Flagellation of Christ* begun by Veronese and finished by his school, as well the *Baptism of Christ* attributed to Veronese.

CHIESA DI SAN SALVADOR

Address: San Marco, Campo San Salvador
ACTV Stop: Rialto
Opening Times:
10 A.M.–12 P.M./5–7 P.M.

This very ancient building was altered several times over the centuries before assuming its present appearance in the sixteenth century when it was completely rebuilt. The building was initially redesigned by Giorgio Spavento, continued by Tullio Lombardo and finished by Sansovino in 1534, thus bringing to a close one of the oldest and most controversial contruction prjoects in the history of Venetian architecture. The façade was built by Giuseppe Sardi in 1663. There are two outstanding works by Titian in the church, as well as sculptures by Alessandro Vittoria and Tommaso Lombardo da Lugano, paintings by Palma il Giovane and Francesco Vecellio, brother of the more famous Titian, who also painted the organ doors which were designed by Jacopo Sansovino.

THE BAROQUE ERA

BASILICA DI SANTA MARIA DELLA SALUTE

Address: Dorsoduro, Campo della Salute
ACTV Stop: Salute
Opening Times: 8 A.M.–12 P.M./3–5 P.M.

Baldassarre Longhena started work on the building in 1631, and the church with its imposing dome is the best-known and most sensational piece of baroque architecture in Venice. The design, one of eleven submitted,

marked the young Longhena's debut and established him as a professional architecture. The church is built on a central plan with a continuous circular aisle onto which is grafted the presbytery with its two semi-circular apses. Just le Cour's high altar is here and contains the venerated twelfth-century icon, the *Vergine Mesopanditissa*. There are marvelous works of art over the altars and in the sacristy, with paintings by Luca Giordano, Palma il Giovane, Sassoferrato and Tintoretto. It is Titian, however, whose powerful works dominate the church with the thirteen masterpieces from the now dissolved monastery of Santo Spirito. The most outstanding of these is the *Descent of the Holy Spirit* altarpiece, already redolent of the proto-baroque spirit, together with the early *Saint Mark Enthroned Between Saints*, in the sacristy.

SCUOLA LEVANTINA

Address: Cannaregio 1149, Calle del Ghetto Vecchio
ACTV Stop:
Ponte delle Guglie

Opening Times: Museum:
10 A.M.–4:30 P.M.; from 1 June
10 A.M.–7 P.M.
Synagogue: 10:30 A.M.–5:30 P.M. (guided tours every hour), admission charge.

Erected between 1683 and 1700 after Longhena, the Scuola appears all the more imposing beside the rugged buildings by which it is surrounded. The rhythm of the façades is animated by alternating pronounced *specchiature* and large curved windows. The main entrance is on the side, where a curved *liago*, the typical Venetian bow window, enlivens the exterior and lights the interior. Inside, above the main chamber, there is the simple women's gallery with its wooden grill. The holy ark manages to combine the exigencies of the Hebrew faith with an orientalized yet wholly Venetian taste for polychrome marbles.

FARMACIA AI DUE SAN MARCHI, SEE CA' REZZONICO

ANTICA FARMACIA A SANTA FOSCA

Address: Cannaregio, 2233
ACTV Stop: Ca' d'Oro or San Marcuola
Opening Times:
9 A.M.–12:30 P.M./3:30–7 P.M.

Still operating on the original site in Fosca, this ancient pharmacy contains splendid seventeenth-century fittings.

CHIESA DEI GESUITI O DI SANTA MARIA ASSUNTA

Address: Cannaregio, Campo dei Gesuiti
ACTV Stop: Fondamente Nuove
Opening Times:
10 A.M.–12 P.M./4 P.M.–6 P.M.

Erected in the twelfth century by the Order of Crucifers, the church passed to the Jesuits and was rebuilt by the architect Domenico Rossi between 1715 and 1728. The façade is magnificently decorated, while the interior has a rich collection of paintings and sculptures, some of which were retrieved from the earlier building. There are works by Gerolamo Campagna and Jacopo Sansovino and paintings by Tintoretto, Palma il Giovane,

and Pietro Liberi, but the greatest of them all is Titian's night scene, the *Martyrdom of Saint Lawrence*. The ornate baroque high altar is the work of Fr. Giuseppe Pozzo, brother of the more famous Andrea.

SCUOLA GRANDE DEI CARMINI

Address: Dorsoduro, Campo Santa Margherita
ACTV Stop: Ca' Rezzonico or San Basilio
Opening Times: 9 A.M.–12 P.M./3–6 P.M., closed Sunday, admission charge

Begun by Francesco Cantello in 1627, the building was completed between 1668 and 1670 by Baldassare Longhena, who imbued it with his own classical and solemn baroque style. The façade overlooking the *Rio Tera* is characterized by two rows of coupled engaged columns, while the façade towards the church is more austere, with a double line of windows intersected by pilaster strips, and standing on a rusticated plinth. Inside, there is a beautiful airy vaulted staircase which is an integral part of a sixteenth- and seventeenth-century installation culminating in a series of paintings by Tiepolo begun in 1739.

CA' ZENOBIO

Address: Dorsoduro 2593-97, Fondamenta del Soccorso
ACTV Stop: Ca'Rezzonico or San Bailio
Admission strictly by telephone request (Tel. 522 8770)

The imposing baroque mass of the palace on the Rio dei Carmini, built by

the architect Antonio Gaspari between 1690 and 1700 for the Zenobio family, is probably the only building in Venice that shows any clear evidence of Bernini and Borromini. The façade progresses horizontally and is enlivened at the center by a curvilinear Roman pediment which relieves the regular rhythm of the attic windows, and by a classical *serliana* which opens over a long, picturesque balcony. A fine collection of paintings was commissioned for the palace, first works by Dorigny, then Gregorio Lazzarini's *Ceres and Bacchus* ceiling, then works by Tiepolo, who painted a series of canvases recounting the story of Queen Zenobia which has since been broken up and sections of which can be found in various public and private collections. Now the building is the headquarters of the Collegio dei Padri Mechitaristi Armeni.

THE EIGHTEENTH CENTURY

PALAZZO LABIA

Address: Cannaregio 275, Campo San Geremia
ACTV Stop: Railway station or Guglie
Opening Times: Wednesday, Thursday and Friday 3–4 P.M. Advance booking necessary, telephone Labia Services (Tel. 524 2812)

The Palazzo Labia is a fine example of late baroque architecture, with powerful Longhenian overtones, built during the early eighteenth century for the family of the same name who were of Catalan origin. Alessandro Tremignon was responsible for the façade on the Campo San Geremia and the building was completed circa 1720 by Andrea Cominelli, who was also responsible for the two waterside elevations. The classic Sansovinian motif of the double row of orders, used for the two *piani nobili* is taken from

Longheni, as is the powerful rusticated ground floor and the *oculi* of the attic floor, punctuated by heraldic bas-relief eagles. There are magnificent frescoes by Tiepolo and Alessandro Mengozzi, known as Colonna, who was responsible for the architectural *quadratura*. The most famous of all depicts Antony and Cleopatra's banquet, central to the narrative pictorial sequence, where Tiepolo seems to be referring proudly and nostalgically to Venice's great sixteenth-century achievements, borne out by the mores and the architecture, and clearly derivative of Veronese. Very little is left of the sumptuous furnishings: there was a major auction in the early 1960s that dispersed the magnificent collections of Carlos de Beistegui, who was the last private owner of the palace. The building is now the regional headquarters of the RAI, the Italian Radio and Television Company.

SCUOLA GRANDE DI SAN GIOVANNI EVANGELISTA

Address: San Polo 2454, Campiello della Scuola
ACTV Stop: San Tome
Admission strictly by telephone request (Tel. 718 234)

An imposing mass of buildings comprising not only the Renaissance palace but also the church dedicated to St. John the Evangelist that overlooks it. Pietro Lombardo's remarkable late fifteenth-century marble *septo* with its curvilinear tympanum links the two buildings, skirting the atrium of the

Scuola to form a kind of open-air hall. Inside there are fine works by Guarana, Domenico Tintoretto, Santa Peranda, Jacopo Marieschi and Morleiter, and the Chancel and the Sala della Croce contain colored stucco work by Francesco Re and others from the second half of the eighteenth century. Once decorated with paintings by Titian, the *albergo* still contains four canvases by Palma il Giovane and a hieratic, rather Byzantine thirteenth-century triptych by a follower of Paolo Veneziano.

CHIESA DI SANTA MARIA DEL ROSARIO O DEI GESUATI

Address: Dorsoduro, Zattere ai Gesuati
ACTV Stop: Zattere
Opening Times: 8 A.M.–12 P.M./5–7 P.M.

Built for the Dominicans by Giorgio Massari between 1726 and 1736, the church rises up from the Zattere, its tripartite façade bearing Corinthian columns and crowned by an innately Palladian tympanum. The main body of the church is gently curvilinear with frescoes executed by Tiepolo between 1737 and 1739, and is the first true example of grand style decorative work.
The church also contains another of

Tiepolo's masterpieces with the altarpiece representing the *Virgin with Saints Catherine of Siena, Rosa of Lima and Agnes of Montepulciano*, which was commissioned in 1740 and executed in a classical and solemn style, quite different from the impetuous frescoes completed the year before. In the third chapel on the right, there is a very high and very austere, almost monochrome, eighteenth-century painting of *Saints Vincenzo Ferreri, Giacinto and Lodovico Bertrando* by Giambattista Piazzetta. The church's magnificent collection of paintings also includes altarpieces by both Tintoretto and Sebastiano Ricci.

PALAZZO A SAN POLO

A private home not open to the public. For security reasons the owners do not wish to divulge the address.

CA' REZZONICO

Address: Dorsoduro 1336, Fondamenta Rezzonico
ACTV Stop: Ca' Rezzonico
Opening Times: 10 A.M.–4 P.M., closed Friday, admission charge.

The palace was designed by Baldassarre Longhena in 1667 and completed in 1758 by Giorgio Massari, who added an extra floor. Massari also took charge of the interior, commissioning artists such as Tiepolo, Giambattista Crosato, Giacomo Guarana, and the quadraturist Pietro Visconti to decorate the salons. The vocabulary of the traditional tripartite design inspired by Sansovino is highly sculptural. The two *piani nobili* rising from a rusticated plinth have large cambered arched windows decorated with masks and sculptures in the extrados. The attic is pierced by articulated *oculi* with short fluted pilaster strips. Originally owned by the Rezzonico family, the building went through several different owners, one of the most notable being the poet Robert Browning, before finally becoming the home of Count Hirschel de'Minerbi. During the 1930s the palace was regularly rented to Cole Porter during the summer months, and was acquired by the Venetian Municipality in 1935. The collections of eighteenth-century furnishings, objets d'art, sculptures and paintings belonging to the Museo Correr, which are among the finest of the nation's treasures, were originally destined for other rooms, such as those in Tieoplo's villa at Ziango and the Farmacia Ai Due San Marchi, which have been recreated here in a magnificent reevocation of the glittering and magical world of the final incomparable years of the Serenissima.

PALAZZO PISANI MORETTA

Address: San Polo 2766, Calle Corner
ACTV Stop: San Tomà
Private, no admission

The palace, built during the fifteenth century, is typically late Gothic, its airy tracery reminicent of the Palazzo Ducale. The two ogival portals indicate the presence of high-ranking families on the two *piani nobili*. "Moretta" denotes the line of Pisans descended from Almorò, the founder of the family in the fourteenth century, and derives from a steady linguistic corruption of his name over several centuries. Inside there is an austere staircase by Andrea Tirali and works by Guarana, Zanchi, Angeli and Tiepolo. The palace passed into the hands of the Giusti counts during

the nineteenth century and was inherited by its present devoted owners.

BIBLIOTECA DI SAN LAZZARO DEGLI ARMENI

Address: Isola di San Lazzaro degli Armeni
ACTV Stop: San Lazzaro degli Armeni
Opening Times: 3–5 P.M.

There has been a convent on the island since the twelfth century. It was given to the Armenians in 1717, who set about restoring the abandoned buildings. Not even Napoleon's rule managed to unsettle the peaceful and hardworking life of the island, which was a focus for the culture and traditions of the Armenian population. Surrounded by a thick circle of dark cypresses, the Mechitarist monastery is made up of various buildings, amongst which is its church, rebuilt after being completely destroyed by fire in 1883, in which the founder of the order, Manug di Pietro, known as Mekhitar, is buried. There is a fine, varied collection of works of art on the island including works by Palma Giovane and Luca Carlevarijs, Canaletto, Sebastiano Ricci and Tiepolo, whose painting of *Peace and Justice* was commissioned for the Ca' Zenobio, whence it came, between 1730 and 1735.

PALAZZO MINOTTO-BARBARIGO

Address: San Marco 2504
ACTV Stop: Santa Maria del Giglio
Private, no admission

This fine palace belonged first to the Duodo family and then to the Barbarigo family, who joined it onto the adjacent building, thus forming one single palace. It subsequently passed into the Minotto and Martinengo families and then to Antonio Dona dalle Rose who kept his vast collection of pictures there. The façade still shows traces of its Veneto-Byzantine origins, as does the twelfth-century acanthus leaf cornice, but it is characterized by its tall Gothic trefoil windows dating from the fifteenth-century reworking of the façade, which gave the palace its present appearance

and a wooden *liago*. Both the second and ground floors were altered during the eighteenth century. The interior includes splendid Louis XIV walnut doors with curious vine leaf bronze handles, and a family chapel with floors inlaid with rare woods. There is a significant amount of stucco work, antique furniture and furnishings and an eighteenth-century luminaristic ceiling with frescoes by Francesco Fontebasso.

PALAZZETTO PISANI

Address: San Marco 2814, Campo Pisani
ACTV Stop: Accademia
Private, no admission

The Palazzetto Pisani forms a sort of avant-corps to the majestic Ca' Pisani, one of the largest and most prestigious private buildings in the city. Bought by Andrea Pisani in 1751, it was linked to the palace itself and overlooks the Grand Canal. The façade, with its restrained and elegant appearance, is faintly reminiscent of Longhena with the background *specchiature*

and the two centered bifoils on the *piano nobile*. The palazzetto belongs to the Ferri counts, having been inherited from the de Lazara family, and it is here that they keep their fine collections of fittings and furnishings.

PALAZZO GRIMANI

Address: San Polo 2896, Calle del Campaniel or Civran
ACTV Stop: San Toma
Private, no admission

The present building is the result of a reworking of an earlier construction, and it assumed its present appearance during the first half of the eighteenth century. It is believed to be the work of Giorgio Massari because it is similar to other palaces and churches designed by him. The unusual height of the rusticated basement (the mezzanine is also rusticated) is underlined by the imposing watergate which, with the geometric jutting keystone, connects it with the *piano nobile* which is embellished by seven centered windows. The attic floor, delineated by the incisive cornice above and the string course below, does not quite match up to the ambitious *élan* of the two floors beneath it. The building's dry stereometry is indicative of the later neoclassical forms of architecture.

PALAZZO BARBARIGO

Address: San Marco
ACTV Stop: Santa maria de Giglio
Private, no admission

The palace, rising up beside the Grand Canal, is a tall seventeenth-century construction, characterized by two broad superimposed *serliane*. On the mezzanine floor, the magnificent wall covering of delicate rocaille stucco work embellishes the rooms, which have *a terrazzo* floors. The most notable of these bears the Barbarigo and Sagredo family crests, alluding to the marriage between Caterina Sagredo and Gregorio Barbarigo in 1739. In a room on the *piano nobile* there are works by Tiepolo, including the only frescoes remaining *in situ* of the original decoration commissioned from him in 1744–1745. There are two monochrome ornamental panels with female allegorical figures, richly adorned with scrolls and garlands, and the large oval painting *of Time Discovering the Truth* in the center of the ceiling.

Chiesa della Pietà o della Visitazione

Address: Castello, Riva degli Schiavoni
ACTV Stop: San Zaccaria
Opening Times:
9:30 A.M.–1 P.M./3:30–7 P.M.

Built by the architect Giorgio Massari, whose design for the hospital next door was never finally realized, the church has a traditional Palladian façade with four Corinthian columns supporting a classical tympanum. The elevation was only completed in 1906 after a considerable bequest enabled work to resume for the first time since the eighteenth century. Among the works decorating the church is *Supper in the House of Simon* by Moretto da Brescia, an admirable landscape, and frescoes by Tiepolo which culminate in the oval ceiling painting of the *Coronation of the*

Virgin, a lyrical combination of light pastel tones, stunning bright colors, and deep, heavy shades, where the garland of musical angels surrounding the scene also alludes to the *Ospealere*, the virtuous women of the Institute and to the special musical tradition of the church.

Palazzo Mocenigo

Address: Santa Croce 1990–1992, Salizzada San Stae
ACTV Stop: San Stae
Owner: City of Venice (Comune di Venezia)
Opening Times: 8:30 A.M.–1:30 P.M., closed Sunday/holidays.
The Biblioteca del Centro Studi di Storia del Tessuto e del Costume (The Textile and Costume Museum) is open on Tuesday, Wednesday and Thursday 8:30 A.M.–1:30 P.M.

For centuries, the palace belonged exclusively to the Mocenigo family, who provided the Republic with seven doges. The present building was the result of alterations commissioned by Alvise I during the early seventeenth century. The façade on the water bears three superimposed *serliane* linked by long, rather Sansovinesque medallions of a type popular in aristocratic architecture between the late sixteenth and the seventeenth centuries. On the land side, the *serliane* merely appear to denote the living quarters. The elevation onto the *salizzada* stands next to a lower building, possibly the *casino*, scene of gaming and conversation, unusually connected in this case to the main building. The immense edifice with its seven floors contains a peerless collection of furniture and decorative work, with frescoes by Jacopo Guarana, Agostino Mengozzi (known as Colonna) and Antonio Zanetti the Younger.

NINETEENTH-CENTURY ECLECTICISM

Palazzo Belloni Battagia

Address: Santa Croce 1783, Calle del Megio

ACTV Stop: San Stae
Private, no admission

Thought to have been built between 1647 and 1663, the palace may have been erected following the Belloni family's acceptance into the ranks of the Venetian patriciate in 1647.
The design is simple and refined, the single *piano nobile* bearing a pentafoil and two other side windows crowned by segmented tympana, a feature typical of Baldassare Longhena, to whom the project is thought to have been assigned.
Two fine baroque coats of arms, set among the group of central windows, bear the crest of the Belloni family: two half moons and a fesse with a star. The palace belonged to the Battagia until 1804, when it was bought by a rich merchant, Antonio Capovilla, who radically changed the interior, giving it its present neoclassical appearance. The *piano nobile* now belongs to the Istituto per il Commercio Estero (the Institute for Foreign Trade), which has systematically and skillfully restored it entirely.

Ala Napoleonica

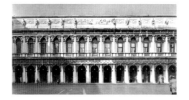

Address: San Marco 76–79
ACTV Stop: San Marco
Owner: Museo Correr (Municipal Museum)
Opening Times: 10 A.M.–4 P.M., closed Tuesday, admission charge

Undoubtedly the greatest neoclassical architectural achievement in Venice, the Palazzo Reale, situated within the Procuratie Nuove, was built for Napoleon's court.
The architect Giovanni Antolini came from Milan to build it in 1897, closely followed by Giuseppe Maria Soli who, with Lorenzo Santi, was responsible for the new façade facing the Piazza called the Ala Napoleonica, or the Napoleon Wing. The attic floor bears a carved frieze with reliefs and statues by Antonio Bosa and Domenico Banti, at the center of which, until the fall of the French government in 1814, there was a painting of Napoleon enthroned as Jupiter.
All the decoration followed the dictates of the Empire style, the rooms decorated with classical Herculean themes using military or floral motifs, small animals, lyrebirds, medallions and grotesques all executed in a typical Venetian vein with small Venetian *vedute* or Lombardic scenes.
Giuseppe Borsato was responsible for most of the paintings, aided by Giambattista Canal, Carlo Bevilacqua the Younger, Pietro Moro, Sebastiano Santi, Odorico Politi and the young, very elegant Francesco Hayez. The Ala Napoleonica now houses the galleries of the Museo Correr.

Palazzo Loredan

Address: San Marco 2945, Camp Santo Stefano
ACTV Stop: Accademia or San Samuele
Opening Times:
Library: 9 A.M.–12:30 P.M./1:30–5 P.M.

The sober architecture of the façade, developed lengthwise and bearing a large quadrefoil, gives no hint of the austere vastness of the atrium that runs the entire depth of the building. This façade on the *campo* was built in 1536 and the new wing on the right-hand side was added in 1618 by Giovanni Grapiglia in a style heavily influenced by Scamozzia. General Illiers, the first

French governor of Venice, took up residence in the palace in 1809, and he commissioned Carlo Bevilacqua the Younger to produce a cycle of Napoleonic frescoes which were painted over only a few years later when the Hapsburgs returned to power. The Istituto Veneto di Scienze, Lettere ed Arti (Venetian Institute of Science, Letters and Art) now has its headquarters in the palace.

TEATRO LA FENICE

Address: San Marco 1965, Campo San Fantin
ACTV Stop: Santa Maria del Giglio or San Marco

The young architect Giannantonio Selva won the competition held to design a theater in Campo San Fantin and began work in 1790, completing the building two years later. The new building was named after the phoenix, a mythical bird that rises rejuvenated from its own ashes. The simple neoclassical façade is distinguished by a fine colonnaded atrium and the handsome Empire-style Sale Apollinee inside, destined for the Philharmonic Society of the same name. The theater, which was the scene of Rossini's retirement from the Italian stage with his final production of *La Semiramide*, was destroyed by fire in 1836. It was rebuilt the following year by the brothers Giambattista and Tommaso Meduna.

CAFFE FLORIAN

Address: San Marco 5659, Procuratie Nuove
ACTV Stop: San Marco

Opening Times: 9 A.M. to midnight, closed Wednesday

Built by Lodovico Cadorin and inspired by the elegant architecture of the eighteenth century, the Florian is eclectically decorated, with huge, rather oriental crystal and painted glass *specchiature,* outlined in mahogony and bronze. The café's history is inexorably bound up with many celebrated personalities. It had always been a literary salon and was much favored by Canova. During the years of Hapsburg rule it became the meeting place of Daniele Manin and his band of conspirators, where they plotted against the occupying forces. During the second half of the last century its tables were graced by all the most famous names of the *beau monde* and the international cultural set, from Proust to Whistler, from Rilke to Monet and even Gabriele d'Annunzio and Eleonora Duse.

CASA FROLLA
ALLA GIUDECCA

Address: Giudecca 50
ACTV Stop: Zitelle

The most exclusive of the Venetian *penzione*, with its cosy and original ambience, is hidden away inside an ancient little palace on the edge of the Giudecca.

PALAZZO DANDOLO

Address: San Marco, Riva degli Schiavoni
ACTV Stop: San Zaccaria

Built towards the end of the fourteenth century, this vast Gothic building lies not far from the Palazzo Ducale. It belonged to several different patrician families over the centuries, until Giuseppe Dal Niel bought the first floor from the Mocenigo in 1840, and the famous story of this well-known hotel began. There are fine frescoes by Jacopo Guarana and the building's tradition of welcoming illustrious visitors dates from the Republican years, when it was often used as a *domus civica*, where important personages visiting the Serenissima were wont to stay.

PALAZZO PESARO DEGLI ORFEI

Address: San Marco 3858, Campo San Beneto
ACTV Stop: Sant'Angelo
Opening Times: 9 A.M.–7 P.M., closed Monday, admission charge

The palace, isolated from the other buildings on the Campo, its grandiose bulk lightened by the long and gracious fifteenth-century flamboyant Gothic multifoil, is quite different from its contemporaries. Thanks to the intelligence and sensitivity of Mariano Fortuny, its last private owner, the feudal and severe syntax of the building has remained unchanged despite conservation work. In addition, the original Gothic layout of the interior remains virtually intact. Thus the courtyard on the side with the wooden additions, so common to medieval Venetian architecture, has been preserved to this day, uncorrupted by the fussy alterations dear to the nineteenth-century imagination. The building is now the headquarters of the Fortuny Foundation and the Museo Fortuny.

TWENTIETH-CENTURY DEBATE

HARRY'S BAR

Address: San Marco 1323, Calle Vallaresso
ACTV Stop: San Marco
Opening Times: 10:30 A.M.–11 P.M., closed Monday

Harry's Bar, one of the most famous restaurants in the world, was fitted into a narrow space hidden away in a modest nineteenth-century building close to the Piazza San Marco. It was originally planned as a bar, intended to be elegant but less formal than the great Venetian hotel bars, but it soon gained international repute both for its cuisine and for its remarkable clientele. In 1935 there were four monarchs dotted about at different tables among the other clients: King Alfonso XIII of Spain, Queen Wilhelmina of Holland, King Paul of Greece, and King Peter of Yugoslavia. Giuseppe Cipriani's innovative approach to what had hitherto been a very orthodox vision of the "sanctuaries" of the luxury restaurant world revolutionized traditional Venetian cuisine, with his creation of now-famous dishes and cocktails such as the "Carpaccio" and the "Bellini." Cipriani's son Arrigo has continued the traditions of this decidedly unique place for many years.

HOTEL EXCELSIOR

Address: Lido, Lungomare Marconi 41
ACTV Stop: Casino

Built by the architect Sardi in 1908, this hotel and the nearby Hôtel Des Bains of literary fame became a favorite haunt of aristocratic seaside tourists. The long eclectic polychrome façade reveals traces of the oriental influence so popular in those days. Enlivened by pinnacles and cupolas, rythmic terraces and tapering turrets, it looks out over the sandy shore, an elegant contrast to the famous bathing huts designed by Ignazio Gardella. The building was one of the last in a series of works organized by the Mayor, Signor Grimani and the Minister of Public Works, Ettore Sorger, intended to give an urban structure to the Lido at the beginning of the twentieth century by creating a network of canals and streets alongside which villas and hotels were subsequently built. Apart from being able to claim to having welcomed some of the greatest and grandest members of the *beau monde*, the Excelsior has been at the center of the activities surrounding the Mostra Cinematografica di Venezia (Venice Film Festival) since 1932.

CASA MAINELLA

Address: Dorsoduro 1259, Rio di San Trovaso
ACTV Stop: Accademia
Private, no admission

Casa Marioni, later Mainella, is on the corner of the Rio di San Trovaso and the Grand Canal. The façade, built by Lodovico Cadorin in 1858, is of thick brickwork interrupted only by the marble fascia on the ground floor. Molded terracotta has been used for the portals, arched lintels and centering, inspired by Codussian and Lombardic decoration. The building shows a return to the vocabulary and materials of the Renaissance, chosen for their relative inexpensiveness and ease of work.

NEGOZIO OLIVETTI

Address: San Marco 101, Procuratie Vecchie
ACTV Stop: San Marco
Opening Times:
9:30 A.M.–12:30 P.M./3:30–6 P.M., closed Monday morning

This was Scarpi's first great Venetian architectural achievement, lauded by some as a "masterpiece of contemporary architecture."
The Negozio Olivetti with its long and narrow proportions is an example of Carlo Scarpa's mastery in organizing an internal space where the materials themselves, intricately interwoven, become its focal points.
The Procuratie Vecchie, of which this is a part, range over the northern side of the Piazza San Marco with a double row of ogival windows above the ground floor which has a portico with fifty arches housing shops. The building, erected between 1500 and 1532, has traditionally been attributed to Mauro Codussi, but there seems to be some doubt about this today and the building is now generally held to be by Scarpagnino.

FONDAZIONE QUERINI STAMPALIA

Address: Castello 4794, Rio di Santa Maria Formosa
ACTV Stop: San Zaccaria or Rialto
Opening Times: Museum: 10 A.M.–12:30 P.M./3:30–6 P.M. 16 May to 14 September; 10 A.M.–12:30 P.M. 15 September to 15 May.
Library: 2–11 P.M.

The Querini family was banished from Venice in 1310 and took refuge on the Greek island of Stampalia, which belonged to them and from which they took their surname.
It was this branch of the aristocratic family who commissioned this austere Renaissance building in 1528.
The library contains over 300,000 books, periodicals, manuscripts and precious incunabula, and a magnificent art collections. Scarpa was responsible for the splendid ground floor of the building and the garden, and the Zen influence can be clearly felt.
There are more than seven hundred paintings here, amongst which are canvases by Gabriel Bella and a handsome bequest of works by Pietro Longhi. The superb upper floors boast fine eighteenth- and nineteenth-century decorations and the furnishings displayed among the delicate early neoclassical stucco work evoke the courtly Venetian life of the last few centuries.

CASA A SAN SEBASTIANO

A private home, not open to the public. For security reasons the owners are not prepared to divulge the address.

PALAZZO ALBRIZZI

Address: San Polo 1490, Campo Albrizzi
ACTV Stop: San Silvestro
Private, no admission

Built in several different stages between the sixteenth and eighteenth centuries, the imposing mass of the palace stands, rugged and superb, against the Campiello Albizzi. The architecture is pure Venetian, the austere main elevation with its superimposed *serliane* and the almost total absence of decoration giving away nothing of the splendor of the interior.
The sumptuous stucco work executed in giddy, emphatic late baroque virtuoso style by Abbondio Stazio di Ticino has putti, allegorical figures, and mythological scenes in twisted phitomorphical frames.
Other rooms are decorated in neoclassical style, constituting another aspect of this amazing aristocratic residence which, thanks to the efforts of the noble family who own it, has remained both intact and beautifully conserved.

PALAZZO SERNAGIOTTO

Address: Cananaregio 5723
ACTV Stop: Ca'd'Oro
Private, no admission

Constructed towards the middle of the nineteenth century by the architect Giambattista Benvenuti, the palace overlooks the Grand Canal, on a line with San Giovanni Crisostomo.
The façade, with its coupled arched windows opening out onto elegant balconies supported by elongated corbels, still carries a late neoclassical cipher. The building is characterized by an avant-corps with Doric columns, divided into three by pilasters, above which there is a large terrace.

CASA PINTO A SAN VIO

Address: Dorsoduro 671, Campo San Vio
ACTV Stop: Accademia or Zattere
Private, no admission

The church of Saints Vitus and Modestus was situated in this secluded *campo* before being demolished in 1813, and it was the final destination of a pilgrimage made by the doge and the *signoria* on the patronal feast day to commemorate Bajamonte Tiepolo's failed uprising, which actually took place on 15 June 1310. A few of the original church decorations, an elaborate cross and some paterae, can still be seen on the façade of the family chapel, an eclectic building erected during the nineteenth century by the Biondetti Crovato da Giovanni Pividor family which is now deconsecrated and in domestic use.

INDEX